Adventure

Adventure

An Argument for Limits

Christopher Schaberg

BLOOMSBURY ACADEMIC

NEW YORK • LONDON • OXFORD • NEW DELHI • SYDNEY

BLOOMSBURY ACADEMIC
Bloomsbury Publishing Inc
1385 Broadway, New York, NY 10018, USA
50 Bedford Square, London, WC1B 3DP, UK
29 Earlsfort Terrace, Dublin 2, Ireland

BLOOMSBURY, BLOOMSBURY ACADEMIC and the Diana logo are trademarks of Bloomsbury Publishing Plc

First published in the United States of America 2023

Cover design: Alice Marwick

Cover image: Grand Teton Mountains © skiserge1 / iStock / Getty Images

Library of Congress Cataloging-in-Publication Data

Names: Schaberg, Christopher, author.
Title: Adventure : an argument for limits / Christopher Schaberg.
Description: New York : Bloomsbury Academic, 2023. | Includes bibliographical references and index. | Summary: "What is the meaning of 'adventure' as we enter the second decade of the 21st century, after a global pandemic, social and geopolitical calamities, and accelerating environmental catastrophes? Casting a wide net and examining literary and cultural case studies, Christopher Schaberg reflects on the nature of adventure in our frenetic times"– Provided by publisher.
Identifiers: LCCN 2022060997 (print) | LCCN 2022060998 (ebook) | ISBN 9798765101452 (hardback) | ISBN 9798765101469 (paperback) | ISBN 9798765101476 (ebook) | ISBN 9798765101483 (pdf) | ISBN 9798765101490 (ebook other)
Subjects: LCSH: Schaberg, Christopher. | Adventure and adventurers–Philosophy. | Adventure and adventurers in literature.
Classification: LCC G522 .S35 2023 (print) | LCC G522 (ebook) | DDC 904–dc23/eng/20230208
LC record available at https://lccn.loc.gov/2022060997
LC ebook record available at https://lccn.loc.gov/2022060998

ISBN: HB: 979-8-7651-0145-2
PB: 979-8-7651-0146-9
ePDF: 979-8-7651-0148-3
eBook: 979-8-7651-0147-6

Typeset by Deanta Global Publishing Services, Chennai, India
Printed and bound by CPI Group (UK) Ltd, Croydon, CR0 4YY

To find out more about our authors and books visit www.bloomsbury.com and sign up for our newsletters.

In memory of Peter Martin

There is no other world.

—KIM STANLEY ROBINSON, *The Ministry for the Future*

CONTENTS

REPRINT ACKNOWLEDGMENTS

"Into a Storm Drain" was originally published at *Terrain.org*.

"Little Cyclists" was originally published at *Transformations*.

"We're Already Colonizing Mars" was originally published at *Slate*.

"The Spacefaring Paradox" was originally published at *Slate*.

"Rocket Men" was originally published at *Popula*.

"Space Tourism and Nature Writing" was originally published at *Los Angeles Review of Books*.

Part 1

A Little Adventure Everywhere

Don't expect a straightforward narrative in this book. Adventure doesn't work like that.

*   *   *

There is a scene in the final James Bond film starring Daniel Craig, *No Time to Die*, that follows a spectacular car chase. Craig's Bond is driving a family-style, dusty yellow Toyota Land Cruiser SUV, and is pursued by a swarm of dark-gray Range Rovers and machine-gun-toting motorbikes. One by one, Bond muscles the Range Rovers and bikes out of his way: they flip off cliffs, roll down steep embankments, get clotheslined by tow cables, and are blown up by grenades.

This scene all takes place along a picturesque fiord abutted by a lush rainforest in northern Norway. It is a beautiful drive, if uncomfortably so.

And as they first set out on this drive, it could well be a family trip: Bond, Madeleine Swan (Léa Seydoux), and her five-year-old daughter Mathilde (Lisa-Dorah Sonnet) are in the Land Cruiser. As they are buckling up, the little girl asks, "Where are we going?" Madeleine responds blithely, "We are going on an adventure." It sure was an adventure, even if it's not the one you'd ever want a child to have to endure.

After hearing this line, I started using it half-jokingly on my three-year-old daughter Vera, no matter what we were doing. Grocery shopping? An adventure. Walking aimlessly around the block just to stretch our legs and get some fresh air? An adventure. Looking for roly-polies in the backyard? Definitely an adventure. Going to the sculpture garden in City Park? An adventure! Vera started asking for an adventure every morning; it sounded like: "We going on a *venture* today?" I gradually came to take it seriously; it changed the way I thought about what we might be doing, and what we could find. This both raises the stakes for the day and makes potentially anything a little more exciting. A little adventure everywhere. Just hopefully not with exploding SUVs and gunfire. There's always a limit.

*   *   *

Adventure, adventure, adventure. Everywhere I turn, it seems as if a call to adventure pops up or is foisted upon me. I hear it in the background so many times each day. Perhaps I've just been tuned into it of late, and so I notice it more. Or maybe it's a critical concept that drives—but also trips up, even sends backward—so much of contemporary life. Michael Nerlich, beginning his sweeping historical project *Ideology of Adventure*, notes that his "concern is the glorification of adventure, of the quest for adventure, of the adventurer (that is, of the person who goes out to seek adventure), and this glorification has by no means always existed everywhere" (3). Looking back over nine centuries, Nerlich was tracing the intricate developments in European literature and culture of the concept of adventure and its glorification. These days, it feels like I can spot glorifications of adventure almost anywhere I look—even if it mostly reflects the kind of "bad" adventure that Nerlich was trying to separate from "real" adventure.

But this kind of mass cultural product is exactly what I'm after. By the third decade of the twenty-first century, we're all confused and conflicted about what risks we want to take and those we'd rather avoid. Live on the edge. Push the envelope.

No fear. What is the meaning of "adventure" after a global pandemic, in the midst of social and geopolitical calamities, and in the thick of accelerating environmental catastrophes? It's only by confronting these circumstances that we might figure out some new limits to the concept of adventure—to see what uses it may still have for us now.

* * *

Adventure courses through this book unevenly. It's a fixation, a project, a target, a ruse, an experience. It changes shape, is sometimes overt and other times subtle and hazy. It's been the aim of my reading and writing life, an objective heightened (often uncomfortably) in this time of great acceleration.

As I put this book together, I realized I was looking back over many authors, texts, and subjects that I first read or became interested in at earlier points in my life. Sometimes this would be as random as noticing a title on my bookshelf that I hadn't thought about in decades. Case in point: While waiting for a Zoom meeting to start, I plucked an old copy of Jack Kerouac's novel *Big Sur* from my bookshelf. I hadn't looked at this book since college, when I originally read it—I remember I was working as a lift operator at a local ski hill while home on winter break, and a storm had knocked out the power at the resort, leaving the seats swaying in the wind. I was stationed at the top of the hill, sitting in a rickety hut shivering while waiting for the lift to start moving again. I was reading *Big Sur* to pass the time. But jump forward twenty-five years, and here I am skimming the introduction to the book in a different place and a different moment in time, and I see where I had underlined Kerouac's explanation of how all his novels were really one continuous, basically true narrative with a recurring cast of real characters who were given different fictionalized names in each story; one day, Kerouac hoped to put all his books together and supply every character their real name. While totally different in terms of aesthetics and form, I think this notion of how multiple books could really be one much longer work burrowed into my brain—it's how I understand all the books I've written, too. And this book, *Adventure*, is the latest chapter.

*   *   *

I wanted to write a book about "adventure" because it's a term that I find myself alternately invoking in earnest and sneering at. It can be a motivating and bolstering call to action; it can be a description of an ordinary event that has taken on unexpected dimensions; but it is often a pernicious scheme, or even just a scam. Adventure is sometimes not where you think it is; or it is claimed to be somewhere, exciting and visceral—but closer investigation proves otherwise: it's simualcral, a cheap product—business as usual. And usually, adventure lies closer than one might think.

*   *   *

When I was a teenager, some friends of mine went off to a summer camp in Colorado called Adventure Unlimited. It was a church camp for Christian Scientists, specializing in activities like horseback riding, rock climbing, river rafting, hiking, and so on. The notion of adventure here awkwardly yokes a particular Neoplatonic religious view to a set of identifiable (and desirable) outdoor pursuits. No limits, but challenge yourself against these. When I recently looked up this camp online, to see if it still exists and, if so, how it was marketed, a peculiar slogan appeared right next to the name: "Opening Windows to God." So there's the limit: *windows* imply *walls*, and an *inside* and *outside*—a square, anthropocentric design. The ostensible infinitude of adventure is constrained by an architectural metaphor. So much for infinitude. It turns out that Adventures Unlimited, plural, is also the name of a company in Texas that rents kayaks and canoes to pleasure seekers. This makes me recall the outfit that I myself worked for periodically between 1999 and 2003: Outdoor Adventure River Specialists, or OARS for short. They still take people on rafting and kayak trips all around the world.

But as I think about these mostly luxury outdoor experiences, it strikes me that a river is a good definition of a limit case for adventure: currents, shifting banks and sand bars, water levels, and channels all determine the course of water and how one can—and can't—travel down (or sometimes up) a river. A successful river trip is a respectful exercise in limits. As such, it's an object lesson for adventure. If Western religion often seeks to overcome the bounds of mortality, we might instead adopt something very different: *adventure limited.*

* * *

American Express emails me a promotional campaign, urging me to use my credit card at restaurants, to go on "culinary adventures." Never mind that I could use my AmEx to purchase ingredients at my neighborhood market and have cooking adventures in my own kitchen; these more exotic adventures are clearly *out there*, at expensive restaurants around the world. So often, adventure is just another name for tasteless consumer capitalism.

* * *

"The adventure ends here, boys." I overhear this line in a Harry Potter movie that my older two children, Julien and Camille, are watching. It's midway through the film; the adventure does not end there. When I teach the first Harry Potter book in my children's literature class, we only read the first forty pages or so—up to the point that Harry finds out he's a wizard. There's enough adventure in those pages alone—the whole franchise could be contained in this short story fragment.

* * *

I think I remember Brad Pitt describing how becoming a parent was "an adventure." When I try to root out this quotation, however, I can't find it anywhere—but I do stumble upon an article from 2013 wherein Angelina Jolie describes motherhood as "the greatest adventure of all." In a similar vein, Jay-Z once summed up his philosophy of parenting as such: "We're just guides." The kids, apparently, are the ones having the real adventure.

* * *

Julien is encouraged to be part of an "adventure club" as part of his fifth-grade class in school. He comes home on Fridays with knotted cords hanging from his backpack. After a while, though, I notice that Julien doesn't mention the club anymore, and no new doodads are hanging from his backpack. Apparently, due to a new Covid variant and reinstated restrictions, the club has devolved into each masked kid just having solo time with their computer for an hour. Another foil for adventure: these ubiquitous, crushing screens.

*   *   *

I get more conflicted about "adventure." Sometimes I want to invoke the word, to set a goal or start down a path (or even just to get going on a mundane project, like cleaning up around the house). Other times I see the word used in crass ways to sell a dumb product or justify an appalling endeavor. I keep turning this word over in my head, trying to figure out some useful limits for how to use it, and in what contexts. Then it will surprise me anew, like when Julien and Camille and I attempted to find an independent bookstore in our neighborhood that had moved locations, and after driving over railroad tracks and along a weedy shoulder, and around some sketchy warehouses, there it was. The bookstore owner said, as we stumbled through the front door, "It's an adventure to find us!" *Adventure*: it's always more complicated than it seems at first glance.

*   *   *

"A book is a new adventure." This slogan adorns a sticker on the title page of another book I spontaneously pull off the shelves, *The Birchbark House*, by Louise Erdrich. A boy in silhouette sits in a tree, with an open book and . . . an ice cream cone? In the four corners surrounding this image are, starting from top-right, a cowboy on a bucking bronco; a three-mast sailing ship; a canoe paddled by a conspicuously head-dressed indigenous person in north America; and a twin-propeller airplane, a DC-3 maybe. The signs of colonial erasure and modern progress are here collapsed and concentrated in a bizarre compass—with a child's reading of a book orienting it all.

* * *

For so many adventures, the action is in the interpretation— the discovery is *textual*, overflowing with meaning. This is why I called my first book *The Textual Life of Airports*: I was interested in all the hermeneutic energy that was happening simultaneously within and parallel to the more overt and obvious mechanics and thrust of actual flight. People were flying, but everyone had stories propelling them forward. When Nathan Heller reviewed my book in the *The New Yorker*, somewhat sneeringly at times, the thing that most annoyed me was how he plucked a relatively obscure quotation by Jacques Derrida from my book and repurposed it for his own ends in his article. It seemed like bad journalism, at the very least. But it also encapsulated how Heller had missed the point of my book: it was about the adventure of reading widely and finding unexpected passages as much as it was about plodding through airports on the way to sleek planes.

* * *

In college my professor Peter Olson introduced me to the works of author Barry Lopez. Dr. Olson assigned Lopez's story collection *Field Notes* in a twentieth-century American literature class; in hindsight, this creative addition to the reading list probably inspired me to make my own substitutions to the canon when I started teaching a similar course ten years later. The stories in *Field Notes* blend magical realism with natural history. Each story is an eccentric adventure of the mind, in a world that might just be the same one the reader inhabits. Incidentally, Dr. Olson was the faculty advisor for an outdoor club that I was part of in college: each semester we took a few backpacking and mountain biking trips around the state. (Our club was hardly a formal organization; we just arranged outings, sometimes at the last minute, and included whoever wanted to be part of our little adventures. We also built a simple triangular climbing wall that we snuck into my dorm room; an art major friend sculpted beautiful handholds out of wood. It barely squeezed into my room. Friends would come by to hang upside down for a few minutes between study sessions. We later moved the climbing wall to an apartment in a dilapidated building in downtown Hillsdale, allegedly an upstairs bowling alley in the 1950s, but I lost track of the climbing wall after I graduated. A loss. It makes me think: how much adventure is premised on loss, and lack?) When, many years later, I had the chance to write a few entries for an encyclopedia of environment in American literature, one of the first headings I claimed was for Lopez's seminal text *Of Wolves and Men*. I remembered that Dr. Olson had raved about this book, but I hadn't read it—at least not very closely. What better way to revisit something than to write an encyclopedia entry on it! An adventure in returning.

* * *

In a high school English class we were supposed to read Louise Erdrich's novel *Love Medicine*, but for whatever reason I didn't like the look of this book (yes, I judged it unfairly on its cover), and so I lobbied for our class to be able to choose another novel from the supply closet where all the course texts were stored. My teacher, Mrs. Landry, amazingly went for this ploy: she allowed us to rifle through the books one class period and then vote on which one we'd read. (Adventurous pedagogy, that deferral of authority! Another formative moment in waiting.) Finding Hemingway's *A Farewell to Arms* amid the various books on the shelves, I decided *this* was the book we should read. Hemingway equals adventure, right? My classmates and I rallied around this choice. But I was bored by *A Farewell to Arms*, probably much more than I would have been by *Love Medicine*, and in fact I would realize this in 2001 in my first graduate seminar taught by Linda Karell, a course on collaborative authorship and authority, in which we studied how Louise Erdrich and Michael Dorris wrote together. This was the real adventure: how words make meaning between people, even unknown people to come. In my American literature class in college, I was at first similarly underwhelmed (or truly just baffled) by *The Sun Also Rises*, but after Dr. Olson's lecture I started to get it: the adventure of Hemingway was in the words.

* * *

If Hemingway's reputation (and oeuvre) is often pegged to notions of rugged adventure and strong characters, his stories are often much more elliptical. Take "Wine of Wyoming," which ostensibly follows a hunting expedition and its daily respites in a gritty village in rural Wyoming during prohibition. As a gloss, it sounds promising. But the actual story is in fact an awkward series of drifting bilingual conversations between an opaque American main character and two French restaurant owners. Actual hunting never happens, but is only spoken of indirectly. Furthermore, the main character's hunting partner is both present and yet completely elided—a total mystery person, more a lurker than a point of narrative intrigue. And then the wine of the title: a special gift from the French elder, a winemaker, to the main character, which arrives only very late in the story and ends up a red herring. In short, nothing really happens in this story except that the *reader* has to toggle back and forth between French and English and try to make sense of what, if anything, is going on. The adventure is in the reading. (And, one can only presume, it was also in the *writing* of such a bizarre, shaggy dog short story. Michael Nerlich again: "Well, writing about adventure is to venture in writing.")

I'm interested not so much in rescuing or reclaiming Hemingway as I am in taming the idea of adventure as it gets yoked to this author and his works. The lasting adventures of Hemingway are less overt than pursuits of extreme sports or sensational near-death experiences. The adventures are on the page. (This also is why Hemingway lampoons overt adventure-writing on the very first page of *The Sun Also Rises*.)

*   *   *

In graduate school at Montana State, Greg Keeler would teach me a similar lesson in the novels of Cormac McCarthy: the action was in the language as much if not more so than how it was in the frontier landscapes and rural horrors. When *The Road* was published, I read it in a single terrifying night, then assigned it as part of a special class I taught at UC Davis called Ideologies of Transport. If velocity is the marker of modernity, as Enda Duffy argues in *The Speed Handbook*, then its wreckage might be what's left after postmodernity. The afterburn of a too-fast mass adventure: McCarthy's *The Road* is like a chemical sample of the exhaust.

*   *   *

The New York Times reports on a giant slide in Detroit, quoting Ron Olson, the chief of parks and recreation for the Michigan Department of Natural Resources: "The idea is to create a balance between having an adventurous ride, yet at the same time keep the speed so it doesn't accelerate too much." Here adventure is something to be limited. It's also something achieved using just gravity and an undulating incline, some burlap sacks and wax. I almost want to take my kids and try it. But I don't want to drive that far. I'm trying to drive less, these days. Imagine a city that could utilize an elaborate system of slides as everyday transit routes . . . chutes and ladders, but for real and for all, somehow.

*   *   *

When I was in high school, I took a weeklong course with an organization called the Bay Area Adventure School. This was effectively a training program to be certified to safely facilitate groups on high ropes courses and climbing walls. We learned the appropriate knots; how to use and care for the ropes, carabiners, and other equipment; how to properly fit helmets and harnesses; and so forth. The school was located in a red pine forest—acres and acres of tall trees all the same age, planted in rows in the mid-twentieth century. There was no undergrowth, and the setting gave the days a peculiar timeless if orderly ambience. It was a very tightly run program, and the "adventures" there were hardly restricted to or delimited by the natural landscape. The goals of these activities were confidence building and teamwork. The adventures were psychological, and social. And all so carefully monitored, with literal safety lines running over everything. When I went out to find the Bay Area Adventure School again during the summer that I was writing this book, it was nowhere to be found. Only the lines of tall pines, timber hallways receding into darkness.

*   *   *

When I make an appointment to get an oil change, I receive an email confirmation that says, "Properly maintaining your Subaru is vital for continued adventures." Another email from the dealership a few months later encourages me to upgrade my Forester altogether, in order to "plan for all-new spring adventures." This reminds me of a sign I saw last time I refilled my car's gas tank, at a Marathon station. Above the pump it said: "Fueling road trip adventures." I looked around at the cars and trucks and people lined up for the five-dollar-a-gallon fuel as Ukraine's soldiers attempted to ward off Russian tanks an ocean away.

Chevy Blazer's 2019 model was advertised as "the perfect sporty SUV for all of your adventures." Ford's newer Lightning, meanwhile, promises to "Power your adventures" with an onboard electrical system. The predicament is overwhelming: how stuck humans are in the web of automobility, all in the name of an adventure that is so obviously straining the planet.

*   *   *

I'm driving Vera to school and a large back Toyota pickup truck zooms past me. Emblazoned across its rear window is a sign for *Reel Adventures—Fishing and Hunting Charters*. I appreciate how the pun conjoins a piece of equipment—the fishing reel—with a notion of authenticity. A *real* adventure. None of those fake pursuits or artificial journeys. But then, isn't a chartered trip already admitting some level of distance from the raw encounter, a layer of mediation created by the guide? Adventure is so easily cast about, yet becomes ephemeral when you draw it in and look closely. And so often, it's about paying for something—or getting paid. Of course, a well-chartered trip can also start one on a lifetime of other adventures. But are they real adventures? Or just reel, technically spooled and played out, predictable and photo-ready?

*   *   *

An advertisement on *The New York Times* homepage tries to lure me to a website for high-end watch trading, *chrono24*. A bearded man in a crisp teal polo drives an antique motorboat. A distant shore, sunlit clouds. Above the clouds, a slogan: *Live For Adventure*. There it is again. I click over to learn more about this citation of adventure, to find further extrapolation: "Moments of Adventure. The era is breaking with tradition. There's a shift toward liberation and self-expression. It's the beginning of personal style. Icons are being born that will last forever." From here, I navigate to a menu where I can buy a watch, or sell a watch. What on earth is the idea of adventure doing here? Do we seek adventure to seize time, or should adventures be experiences when time slips away? Who looks at their watch—or values it in dollars, really—in the middle of an actual adventure?

*   *   *

Greg Keeler writes a sonnet every morning, and he sends them out to a small group of friends. A recent one, "My Own Weight," ends with these lines:

The bathtub is
an adventure in itself.

Yes, this is it: a limit for adventure, the closing-in space-time of aging and living with(in) one's own body. A poem, too, is a limit wherein an adventure can happen. Greg has written over two thousand sonnets, and keeps testing, and abiding by, their internal limits each morning.

*   *   *

There is a series of short clay-animated cartoons from the mid-2000s called *Bert and Ernie's Great Adventures*. They played as inserts on Sesame Street episodes, replacing the skits of the old familiar puppets. The shows have captivated my children, and they delight me because of the way they proclaim and create a "great" adventure within the tight bounds of five minutes. Each episode begins with the two buddies tucked in their beds, and Ernie starts singing the theme song:

> *Every night when I lie in bed*
> *I see pictures dancing in my head*
> *Buddy Bert, buckle up and we'll fly away . . .*
> *We're adventuring!*
> *Every time the bed starts tappin'*
> *Something special's gonna happen*
> *My favorite kind of traveling . . .*
> *We're adventuring!*
> *Come along with Bert and Ernie,*
> *We're gonna take a little journey . . .*
> *Bert and Ernie's Great Adventures!*

Each great adventure takes place, in other words, during *sleep*—the "little journeys" are dreams. And not just any dreams but *shared* dreams. Each adventure lands the duo in a new place and time: in the desert with a magic lamp and a genie, at the seashore with a friendly octopus, in a rubber ducky-shaped spaceship en route to the moon (which turns out to be inhabited by Bert-shaped moon-men). And all the while, Bert and Ernie contain and share these adventures within each five-minute framework. With pithy TV content like this, who needs sprawling cerebral films like *Inception* or *Dr. Strange in the Multiverse of Madness*?

One episode finds Bert and Ernie as ecologists in a forest that is being devoured by a voracious anthropomorphic (and operatic) beaver. They have to teach the beaver not to fell and chew *every* tree but to instead coexist peacefully with the other inhabitants of the forest. This particular episode, as silly and short as it is, gets at the heart of a dilemma, for me: how is adventuring yoked to environmental awareness, and ecological cross-species responsibility? Of course, it's over before we can think these thoughts out to any social or scientific application. On to the next great adventure, another shared dream, in the following episode. But what if we were able to articulate and embrace the great adventure as a truly shared dream? And then, awaken the dreamers while keeping the adventure alive? We have arrived at—as Giorgio Agamben writes in quite another context, but which seems to apply here—"the threshold through which the animal becomes a man and man becomes an animal again. Passing this threshold is the adventure of adventures" (81).

*   *   *

In her memoir *I Came All This Way to Meet You*, Jami Attenberg writes about a visit to Hong Kong, in the midst of which she embarks on a day trip to a mysterious destination: "I was on a goddamn adventure. This is a strange thing I am doing, I thought. I have already gone so far away from home. And now, for some reason, I needed to go even farther" (220). Attenberg gets at multiple competing impulses around the idea of adventure, here. Adventure can spur one to a remote place, and it can motivate one to go *beyond* the place. Into what is *strange*. This makes me think about Agamben again: "the stranger and riskier the adventure, the more desirable it becomes" (25). But I wonder, what is the threshold of this yearning? Must adventure finally consume the adventurer? Or can this energy of the pursuit be turned back on itself, inward and at home? In a way, Attenberg's book hints at the latter. But this is a great challenge for adventure, not just for individuals but for the cultures and masses that seek this elusive object. It might be closer than we realize, that place or experience we were after all along.

*   *   *

I'm at the New Orleans airport for the second time since the Covid pandemic began, on my way to Missoula, Montana, to present part of this book. I file through a long security line, snaking past the same placid passengers six times before arriving at the checkpoint. Past security, the smells of fried food wash over me. Everywhere, an ambience of slight unease—of the normal on edge. I'm not one minute down the C concourse when I see it flash on a big screen over a bar: SIX NIGHT ADVENTURES. It's an ad for a cruise line.

On our ascent out of New Orleans, I look down and see hundreds, probably thousands, of dotted blue tarps stretched over roofs: unrepaired damage from Hurricane Ida. Now *that* was an adventure—though it feels both right and wrong to call it that.

Landing in Denver, all is pandemonium. The food courts are glorified feed troughs. The sound is deafening. Everyone is moving so much faster than I remember. This airport has long concourses that invite ambling and staring out at the tarmac and horizon. But everyone is hustling. The bathrooms resound like boisterous locker rooms, people shouting about piss and shit and guffawing. Most power outlets don't work, and passengers walk around zombie-like, phones in hand with charging cords dragging behind them. Around one silver column, I notice that someone has plastered simulacral stickers of power outlets—a perfectly cruel prank, sending up our collective craving for constant adventure at our fingertips.

On my second leg, my seatmate leaves the entertainment screen on the default United channel, even though she is not watching it (and you *can* simply turn them off) and out of the corner of my eye I keep seeing the word over and over in a two-hour loop: *We carry a sense of Adventure. And a Free*

Checked Bag. We are the explorers. United Airlines. . . . We seek adventure. We are the explorers. United Airlines. Around me, passengers gaze at their phones, or watch action-adventure films on the small screens in front of them, or doze. Adventure at its apex, and at its nadir.

When I arrive in Missoula, it is incredibly dark outside—and I realize I haven't seen darkness like this since I was in Michigan last summer. But it even feels darker than that. My host Gillian Glaes picks me up and explains it's a brand-new airport, so she's not exactly sure how to find the way out of the parking lot. We pass long lines of minivans, Blazers, F150s, and Subarus. Signage is sparse, and circuitous. For the first time today, I actually feel like an explorer, on an adventure: it is limited, and more real for it.

*   *   *

A winter email from the Department of Natural Resources in Michigan offers a new interactive map, to help me find "ideas for new frosty adventures all around the state." I get these emails because I purchase annual fishing licenses from my home state, where I return each summer. The book I wrote before *Adventure* was called *Fly-Fishing.* It was about my long obsession with fly-fishing, and how I practice it in a minor way, in waters close to home. But as I wrote the book, and as I reflected on it after it was done, something nagged at me: the disconnect between the actual act of fishing and the recording of it, the thinking back on it and writing about it later. The real adventure was always *out there*, beyond or before the page. I attempted to bring the writing and the fishing closer and closer together, as I worked on the book—but this distance can only get so proximate. Something I tried after the book was done was to think about everything that happens in the run-up to one of my fly-fishing outings. The pre-adventure, as it were. This is what it looks like:

We used to meet at 5:00 a.m. Then it crept back to 4:45. Then 4:15. The goal is always to be out in the water before even the first glimmers of dawn. The earlier, the better. My fishing buddy Glen has a longer drive from his house—anywhere from forty minutes to an hour, depending on road construction, fog, and deer. From my house, it's just seven minutes to the parking spot, off a two-track in the national lakeshore. I typically get there first, but within minutes I'll see his headlights angling down the road. Sometimes we meet at the last intersection and drive the last mile as a caravan of two.

Morning fishing trips are something of a cliché. But the magic that can happen in these hours is real—and a subtle adventure is hidden in the details, before the fishing even starts.

Cars parked, we step out into the silence and greet one another, our shared excitement palpable in the air. Owls hoot off in the woods. We open the back hatches of our cars to get our waders on and assemble our gear. By that point I've gulped down a thermos of black tea, and I need to pee once more before pulling on my waders. Needing to go when standing chest-deep in water, with no solid ground around to speak of, is another type of adventure I prefer to avoid.

I step out of my flip-flops and put on thin Smartwool socks. The layering debate happens at this point. It might be thirty-nine degrees now, but it will get up to eighty degrees in a few hours. A fishing shirt under a windproof but light jacket should be enough, but a fuzzy fleece collar would be nice. No rain in the forecast this morning—Orion is still leaning brightly on the horizon—so we don't need our waterproof jackets. But we can see our breath in the air and so we add an extra layer for now on top. We don't need fleece pants under our waders, though, because at this point in the summer the lake is like bath water. It will be one of those odd inverted mornings where the air is chilled and the water steams up from beneath—and the fish themselves are eerily warm, when we hold them for a moment before releasing.

We pull on our waders, then loosen laces and jam our feet into the stiff boots—rigid from repeated submersion and drying. I got these boots a few years ago from Patagonia and love them; the tagline on the box was "The last boots you'll ever need to buy." A solid guarantee, or an ominous innuendo hinting at a final adventure ahead? Never mind; I tie my laces with a square knot and double knot them, then clip my waders' boot-covering over the frontmost lace. Wiggle my toes to make sure everything is in place and stomp a few times before we head down the trail to the water. I clip my waist belt and adjust the shoulder straps, clicking everything into place. I put my wallet, phone, and car keys in the interior zip pocket of my waders—safe from water, as long as I don't go too deep.

I have a lightweight fishing vest with four exterior pockets for what I need. In each larger pocket, a fly box: one for surface patterns (most in green and black) and one for subsurface minnows (chartreuse and white, plus a few darker ones). In the left front pocket, I have three thirty-yard coils of monofilament line: one 10lb-test, one 15lb-test, and one 25lb-test. These I can tie together to create a tapered leader and tippet, or just replace parts as needed. I have my nippers (like simple nail clippers) for cutting line, dangling from a retractable cord on my chest. And my pliers for removing deep or otherwise awkwardly set hooks, looped on an old piece of fly line and tucked in a pouch inside my vest, so I don't snag my fly line on the handles. The pliers also have a line clipper built in, behind the gripping clamp. Everything here is about keeping loose ends at a minimum. This particular vest has a design flaw, though, where the straps to tighten it around the base of my rib cage tend to hang out and can grab the line when I'm casting, so I have to wrap all the excess strapping around itself and make it snug. (I should probably just cut off the excess, seal the tag end, and be done with it; I rarely need to adjust it too much.) I can put a water bottle in a backpack compartment of the vest, and I also have my old river knife clipped to a side strap, in case I ever need to cut something in a hurry. I have three steel bite guards with clips at the end, to use when we go after pike—pike are like freshwater barracuda, long and muscular and their mouths full of rows of razor-sharp teeth. And a small fabric sleeve that goes over my index finger, for stripping line and to protect the finger when the line gets pulled out quickly by a fish. I usually tuck a granola bar, or a bag of nuts and dried fruit, in the back pouch with the water bottle. All this is organized the night before, so I just have to slip the vest on over my light jacket.

Glen doesn't like to fish with a vest, and instead just slips his fly boxes or even just plastic bags of flies he has tied into his waders. Sometimes this means he ends up with a fly that works its way down a leg and under his foot, and he wades and fishes while worrying that he will get a hook in his toe, or that it could puncture his waders and let water in. So he winces and tiptoes around in the water all day. Glen has a final argument with himself about whether to bring his net. I always tell him not to. Sometimes he still does.

Fully dressed, now comes the truly hard decision: what rods and reels to take with us. If we know we want to go for the biggest fish (pike and big bass), or if it's really windy, we might opt for our 9-foot 8-weight outfits. With these we can throw the largest flies and contend with gusts. But it means we will forfeit any chances to target smaller fish—and sometimes that's even more challenging. So we could take our 9-foot 6-weights, which can be used for larger fish *or* for smaller ones. Or sometimes, when we know the bluegill are active, we opt for our 7-foot 3-weights, which are dainty and extremely fun with even the smallest fish. Our 8.5-foot 5-weights seem to get used less and less these days. Glen and I never discuss the fact that we always fish with the same weight rod and line as the other, but invariably we do. It's a tacit solidarity.

Today we choose our 6-weights, as we want to try some chunky poppers that Glen tied, and which would be all but impossible to cast on anything smaller. Glen hands me a fly whose artificial eyes glow a reflective metallic red. I tie it to the end of my tippet in the dark, holding the eyelet of the hook against the dim light of the back hatch. It's a knot I know by muscle memory, luckily.

All of this is done by the backs of our Subarus, barely aglow. I have to remember to switch my hatch light off manually, because it's not automatic.

When we're all done, we close the backs of our cars; then we are plunged into darkness. The sky is ink. And it is about to get darker when we head into the woods for a short trek to the lake—over a hill, through a pine grove, across some wild ground berry patches, and into the swamp before the water opens up.

All suited up, we lock our cars, thumbing our key buttons in their interior pockets, two beeps and corresponding blinks of yellow tail lights, and we start walking toward the edge of the forest. This has all taken as little time as possible.

The entrance to the trail is invisible from the dirt road. You have to know where it is: right when you're at the trees a little opening reveals itself, and we slip between a maple tree and a white pine, and head into the woods. Walking with a 9-foot fly rod you have to hold it steadily and carefully so as not to inadvertently get hung up on a branch or, worse, snap off the rod tip. Some people walk with the rod tip trailing behind, so it naturally follows your lead. I prefer to point the rod directly in front of me, and just aim for where I want to go, and trust that it all works out. (So far I've been lucky, though I did get hung up in a barbed-wire fence once in Mid-City, New Orleans, on my way to fish in Bayou St. John. An adventure for another time.)

Each step counts. It's easy to walk off the trail, get lost or even momentarily disoriented. And then everything gets thrown off. I can't tell you how many fishing trips have been botched because of an early bungle. I am not a superstitious person, and yet I fall into all sorts of reflective pitfalls and worrying traps when I am on my way to the lake. So much can go wrong: something forgotten in the car, like when Glen forgot his sunglasses and battled surface glare all morning. Or you step on a dagger of beaver chew and it slices right through your waders—the day is over before it begins. (I did this on the Gallatin River once, in Montana.) Or a pack of coyotes starts yipping not too far away, maybe really close actually—giving the day an unnerving mood. One time we passed into the clearing just as a pair of nighthawks were diving and circling near the edge of the shore. They were silent scary invaders simply devouring insects, swooping around us as we dodged and feinted our way to the water.

Pine needles cushion and crack underfoot. Puddles from the last rain appear depthless in the dark. All the crepuscular creatures are out with us: racoons, skunks, opossums, porcupines. They sound enormous in the undergrowth. Just getting to the lake in these black woods is its own adventure. Once we're out on the water, the stars and moon will brighten things—but under the beveled canopy, it is darker than dark.

Coming out of the woods and into the clearing by the water, our eyes adjust. At the water's edge, what in the daytime is straightforward presents itself as an abyss. The line between lake and land is invisible and has to be felt with careful feet. Water snakes glide in and out of the reeds. Around this time, the first robins are starting to sound off in the oak trees. They almost warn, *Stay ashore!*

Stepping from one element into another, in the dark, requires more than a leap of faith. Fortunately we know these waters enough to wade right in, but even so, depending on where we are, we sometimes find ourselves sinking in silty quicksand. We wade out past the sedges and cattails, away from the dogwoods, starting to strip line from our reels for the first casts. I move twenty feet away from Glen, and we instinctively settle on two different areas to focus on. We see circles where fish are rising. Still an hour or so to go before sunrise. We're almost fly-fishing now. The adventure I bought my license for is about to happen. But really, it already commenced an hour ago.

*   *   *

Vera's plastic Mickey Mouse backpack comes with a fake walkie-talkie that shouts in Mickey's voice, "We've got everything we need for an adventure!" The pack includes nonfunctioning binoculars, a working (if rather dim) flashlight, an oversize jackknife with a dull plastic serrated blade and a two-inch ruler, as well as a play compass. These items gradually get strewn around the house, under sofas and behind bookshelves—having their own adventures, as it were.

*   *   *

The University of California at Davis, where I earned my
doctorate, invites me to join a small group travel program
for alumni called Aggie Adventures. A recent package offers
"deluxe accommodations" at Apex City Quay Hotel & Spa
in Dundee, Scotland, to play golf and visit nearby castles. It's
funny, because UC Davis was where I became suspicious of
such adventures. I was writing about airports as fascinating
places in themselves—looking aslant at the desires that drive
air travel, and at the liminal times that so often get brushed
over in favor of gleaming destinations. My Aggie Adventure,
such as it was, entailed getting lost in airports in books and
films and artworks for six years, and writing about it.

                        *   *   *

I find myself encouraging an author friend to consider a
"choose your own adventure" approach to an unwieldy book
manuscript that she is working on. What do I even mean by
this, though? Could *I* pull off such a feat? When you look at
the original Choose Your Own Adventure books, they're not
exactly models of narrative genius. Thin plots, absurd premises,
binary choices, and all too quick resolutions. Leslie Jamison
attempted to redeem the Choose Your Own Adventure legacy
in a recent *New Yorker* article, but her adoption of the form
came off as precious—as much as I appreciated the reporting
and the story. What would it mean to really construct a book
that would leave the reader to find their own paths, reading
improvisationally or by some other ad hoc method? Actually,
my colleague and great friend Mark Yakich achieves this with
Thoreau's journals, opening at random or sometimes turning
to whatever date it is in the present moment, just backward
170 years. I tried it, and what do I find?

On May 29, 1857, Thoreau contrasts an American tendency
to be hired to be adventurous, with the propensity to set out
on one's own "bark" to find an authentic adventure. In other
words, Thoreau saw how adventure was increasingly being
tied to capitalist productivity, which, curiously, seemed to
Thoreau like "doing nothing." Instead, we should "run down

the coast on a voyage of adventure or observation on [our] own account." Here, as in other places in Thoreau's writings, the Romantic impulse for self-reliance is internally snagged, entrapped by the patterns of life that give rise to this fantasy: exploration, a philosophical notion of complete selfhood, the fraught ideals of industry and "accounting"— all these things muddle the aspirations of the American transcendentalist who seeks as-if pure adventure. My home state adopted the slogan "Pure Michigan" a while back—another residue of this complicated Romantic idealism.

*   *   *

A newlywed couple in the first episode of the HBO show *The White Lotus* embarks, in the revolting husband's plucky words, on "the adventure of a lifetime." The eponymous lead character of Netflix's *Emily in Paris* announces her new job opportunity abroad as "an adventure." I wonder, how many television shows these days start this way, with the invocation of an adventure? It's especially odd to think about in the age of binge-watching, when indulging in a show can feel more thrilling, and addictive, even transgressive, and ultimately exhausting than ever—yet these shows must and do end, leaving one in a mental fog, the adventure ephemeral twice over.

*   *   *

A new Lego set drops, the Ultimate Adventure Castle: a Disney-themed building with five princesses (Ariel, Moana, Rapunzel, Snow White, and Tiana), each with her own room. The ad copy describes that the set is "full of functions and features that let kids play out endless adventures." Another tagline elsewhere on the Lego website asserts that the toy will "Fulfill a child's love of endless adventures." The set combines with other Lego Disney castle sets; it's modular. The subtle shifts across these marketing spots intrigue me. Adventure here is something self-contained: it's the "ultimate" castle. But it's also something to be played *out*, away into hitherto unknown realms. And adventure is supposedly something innate, stemming from "a child's love"—indeed, *endless* adventures. The multiple imperatives here are dizzying. Adventure comes across as something out there (in a consumer product), inside the person who builds and plays (the nascent imagination), and across other toys (sold separately). It's also, "warning: a choking hazard." The real adventure is always smaller.

*   *   *

My host during my visit at the University of Montana tells me about a sweatshirt she has that says, READY FOR ADVENTURE. The caption lies beneath the state-shape of Montana, with an inset illustration of mountains, a river, pine trees, a tent, and a campfire. No humans in sight. It's an odd image, at once immediately intuitive and surrealist in fact. The scene is set in the political-geographic boundaries of the state; the scene encompasses the whole state, as if an outsized ego is being satisfied; the scene is tranquil, sparse, depopulated. It is a mixed message for adventure, not to mention readiness: it could be survivalist, touristic, or simply leisure-active.

No matter what, though, it is *colonial.* The shape of the map makes this plain: adventure here means readiness for political statehood, for a specific kind of empowered citizenship. Adventure can't outrun its legacy.

Back home after my trip, Camille runs up to me with a children's dictionary and jabs her finger at a page. "Here, write about this!" I see the entry:

> adventure 1. Something a person does that involves danger and difficulties. Columbus' voyage to the New World was a great *adventure.* That book is about the *adventures* of the pioneers. 2. An exciting or unusual experience. Their first trip by airplane was an *adventure* for the boys.
>
> adventurous 1. Eager to have exciting or dangerous experiences; bold. The *adventurous* campers set off on a canoe trip in the wilderness. 2. Full of danger; risky. The first voyages to the New World were *adventurous* journeys.

Here I am whacked over the head with all the conflicting and contradictory meanings of this word. Adventure might be as simple as an individual sense of *danger* or *difficulty*, or as complex as mass conquest and global economic order. It could just be encountering the *unusual*, or it involves airplanes and all the logistics and energy networks that buttress this form of travel. It may be exciting, taking place on a humble canoe; alternatively, the ships prophesying world domination are on the horizon.

Adventure is completely fraught, stretched taut between the mundane and the exotic, the innocent and the guilty. It might be connective and humbling; or it can be violent, hegemonic. In the accelerating second (or third) century of the Anthropocene, things lean heavily toward the bleaker aspects of adventure. What might it take to recover any positive functions of this concept? Or has the term outlived its use? Are we now finally ready for adventure, or should we be over it, once and for all?

*   *   *

At one point as I was working on this book, I searched through my email inbox for the word "adventure," looking for something I'd written long before, about sport utility vehicles. What I found in some of the earliest messages surprised me:

Greg Keeler wrote to me that my first interview with Loyola would be "an adventure in itself." An administrative assistant in the American Studies program at UC Davis told me that moving to New Orleans would be "a wonderful adventure." A student in the last class I taught at UC Davis thanked me for my "sense of adventure" in how I approached our subject. My late father-in-law winkingly signed off an email to me, after I graduated from my PhD program, with "Professor Bachelor Adventure Martin." Even in my dusty email archives, adventure was percolating.

I gradually realized I had been thinking and writing about adventure for a long time. Whether it had to do with air travel and the desire to fly (away, somewhere else, to a destination) or tracing the idea in books about nature and wilderness, or bellowing from SUV advertising, or nestled in fantasies and realities of space exploration, or even simmering in my own travails to make a home and a life with my family in New Orleans, Louisiana, with summer excursions to the woods of northern Michigan . . . what tied these various (sometimes jostling) things together in my mind was *adventure*. Even teaching literature has been a new adventure each semester, every single class. So I found myself revisiting many pieces of writing I had not understood were connected until now, and attempting to make those connections more intentional as I ranged across happenstance findings—to connect some dots, or at least project a constellation.

What follows is a foray across this field, where I identify and complicate associations with *adventure*. These next two parts are a matter of high contrast: first located around my home and daily life in New Orleans and then going as far as we humanly can (yet), into space. Hold these two extremes in mind.

Part 2

Nowhere Else

Adventures in and out of New Orleans

Watching Hayao Miyazaki's film *Spirited Away* with Vera one afternoon, I was struck by a moment in the opening scene. A family is driving to an unknown new town, and the mood is one of suspense, nostalgia, and low-grade dread. The main character Chihiro sulks in the backseat of the car; she does *not* want to move. Her mother tries to pep Chihiro up: "It's fun to move to a new place. It's an adventure!"

This sentiment appeared again a week later in a 2022 *New Yorker* profile of the late artist Matthew Wong: retrospectively explaining their move to a new city when Wong was an adolescent, Wong's mother is quoted as saying that moving would be "an adventure."

I moved a lot as a kid; it rarely felt like an adventure to me. In my experience, moving was mostly just awkward and unsettling. It disrupted life and made for a lot of uneasiness and social isolation in school—in different schools, as my family picked up and moved to another city in Michigan an hour away from our last home, or eastward across the Midwest all the way to Connecticut, but just for a year, while my father

worked in New York City before being transferred back to the
Detroit area, again. My early years are a blur of these moves.

*   *   *

I've lived in New Orleans for fourteen years now. I have made
a home here with my family. It hasn't always been easy: the
cost of living has gone up considerably since I arrived in
2009, and my salary has been frozen for over a decade due
to budget constraints and financial mismanagement at my
university. Hurricanes threaten every summer and early fall—
and sometimes they hit. An approaching hurricane seems in
the abstract like a kind of adventure. But once it happens, that
register changes abruptly.

Still we've made a life here, my children in a wonderful
public school close to our home in Mid-City, and our house
an oasis in the complex dynamism that is a 300-year-old city
awash with the detritus of the Gulf South. The chatter of
gunfire at night. Sirens and crows exchanging wails. Friendly
shouts from across the street intermingled with the screams of
people being carjacked a few blocks away. Our neighborhood
is in the center of the city, and we hear it all.

But now, as I write this book, I feel like I might be on the
verge of a big life move. For a few years it seemed like a position
might open up for me in Arizona, and I was getting excited
about the idea of moving to the Phoenix area—a parched and
equally vexed but still vibrant place. The possible job ended
up evaporating like so much spilled water on the desert floor,
and so that move was an adventure deferred. But I am keeping
my eyes open to other possibilities, even as I try to make peace
with my relatively settled life on the dirty coast, the ramshackle
yet vivid island-like city of New Orleans. Looking back, now, I
want to archive some adventures of living here. I never kept a
diary, but I wrote enough notes and essays to recreate a partial
timeline.

I've come to know this city (or small slices of it, anyway),
and each summer when I return from our sojourns in northern
Michigan, I relish the humidity and culture, the food and the

soundscape. Even as parts of the city grate at me or seem profoundly dysfunctional, I continue to dwell here—my adventure in living, for the time being.

I look back over these years, trying to piece together this adventure in distended diary form. The limit on adventure here is the mundane, the living in a place through time. Learning from it, tuning in—to feel smaller, at home.

*   *   *

2009: We move to New Orleans, renting a third-floor, two-bedroom apartment in an old Spanish colonial building right off St. Charles, a few blocks from Napoleon Avenue. I can walk to campus in twenty minutes. We live near incredible restaurants tucked into neighborhood blocks. Our apartment is airy and sunny and charming, but has only a window A/C unit that can't cool the place down under eighty degrees. And in the winter, an old gas heater in the center of the apartment never quite seems to turn on—barely more than the pilot flame issues minimal heat. Our landlords are a sister and brother who live in separate apartments on the second floor; they are ninety-six and ninety-four years old, respectively. A nearby mansion has an air conditioning compressor that is so loud that it wakes us up at night.

2010: We buy our first house, an over-100-year-old, 900-square-foot single-shotgun in the Uptown neighborhood. The house is the narrowest version of the single I have encountered in the city: eleven feet wide (most singles are closer to fifteen feet wide). I can walk across Audubon Park to get to campus. Julien is born that summer. A new adventure begins.

2011: I meet the architect Ammar Eloueini at his new project site, where he gives me a tour of his adventurous J-House. It's a house that does a twist in midair, saving ground space by overhanging the earth. (It's hard to describe, but you can Google it.) The building is designed to minimize the footprint (flood zone thinking) while maximizing the use of the geometry at hand. The house is situated on a traditional narrow New

Orleans lot, 30 feet wide by 150 feet deep. The views from the upper floors—the main living area—are striking, with the wide windows ten feet above ground framing the surrounding neighborhoods in effortless, frayed panoramas. There is a stunning sliver of light that cuts gently into the midpoint of the roof. The design makes use of the two overhangs for a carport in the front and a shaded outside area toward the back. The covered spaces have the curious feel of a Zen garden, but one that you would hang out in. It reminds me of walking around a Gehry building, but the difference is that the J-House seems to be inviting me to pull up a chair to the curvy side and open a bottle of wine: to sit down and enjoy the structure while in very close proximity to it. (Gehry's buildings, on the other hand, seem to facilitate *movement*. This is not a critique: they do it really well, for all kinds of movements.)

When I first walked by the J-House a month prior (the house is mid-construction), Lara remarked that it felt like a huge shell you'd find on the beach: startled by its size, perhaps, but familiar with its whorls. Indeed, there is something about the structure that appears accreted, then etched away over time, literally *lived in*. This is interesting given the fact that the house is not yet finished. But it goes to show how much thought has gone into the space: already lived in while yet uninhabited, as it were.

When I go back to the house a week later and stand outside it for a while, just watching the clouds move by overhead, it occurs to me that it also resembles the eroded smoothness of slot canyons in the desert southwest, those little flash-flood grooves that you can stand in and look out of, watching the clouds and sky fly by. In this way, it is vaguely reminiscent of standing within James Turrell's "Three Gems" at the de Young museum in San Francisco. The difference, though, is that unlike one of Turrell's carefully curated skyspaces, the J-House is just nonchalantly *here*, intermingling with myriad other shotgun and creole cottage-style homes on the block. In New Orleans, you get these fractured views of the Gulf Coast sky walking down any street, as the staggered rooflines intersect and morph into one another, occasionally collapsing in on the structures beneath. New Orleans shows off its *erodedness*. The J-House is like a remark of this common experience: it reminds you to take the time to see time at work—mere temporality as an adventure.

Frank Lloyd Wright evoked the power of erosion with Fallingwater, too, which suggests the very foundation of the home as ephemeral, moving, almost Heraclitean in its constant relationship to dynamism. Eloueini seems to be balancing this impulse with the always-already submerged feeling of New Orleans: we're under water, and there's no getting around it. Better to build with time and levity both on the mind, aware of radical flux and the reliable comforts of a home-space, at turns and at once.

I am put in the mindset of Wallace Stevens's poem "An Ordinary Evening in New Haven":

> These houses, these difficult objects, dilapidate
> Appearances of what appearances,
> Words, lines, not meanings, not communications,
>
> Dark things without a double, after all,
> Unless a second giant kills the first—
> A recent imagining of reality,
>
> Much like a new resemblance of the sun,
> Down-pouring, up-springing and inevitable,
> A larger poem for a larger audience,
>
> As if the crude collops came together as one,
> A mythological form, a festival sphere,
> A great bosom, beard and being, alive with age.

Ammar Eloueini is building a house that is truly "a larger poem for a larger audience." It inspires us to think about what we could do with our own small home, if we ever have the chance to renovate it.

* * *

2012: Late August. We wait for a storm, to see what it will do. It's eerie. There's the god's eye view provided by satellites, but this form of "knowledge" is hardly commensurate with the feeling of life on the ground. The planes overhead seem louder than normal, today; maybe one of them is a NOAA Hurricane Hunter. I can't decide if that name—*Hurricane Hunter*—is comical or heroic, an absurd misnomer or an admirable attempt at something more primitive within our techno-media maelstrom. As if we could "hunt" these colossal storms. As if *we* are the ones with power against such force.

Beyond the planes and helicopters chopping above, there's a different kind of buzz outside: the buzz of people stocking up at our neighborhood market, and other people frantically loading their cars in order to evacuate. Some cars drive down our skinny street startlingly fast—panic in action. Other people gab and laugh and stroll down the street with cases of Abita and Miller High Life on their shoulders. We've got our bags packed and the house all tied down—but we're not leaving, at least not yet.

This morning it was dead-still, and the sky was a brilliant azure—I've never quite appreciated the phrase "calm before the storm" until today. Now in the afternoon, the light in the sky is diffuse in a weird way. There isn't exactly a cloud layer yet, but it's as if a sheet of fine linen has been pulled over us. The wind is starting to gust, and I can hear it sporadically whistling through the 100-year-old chimney a few feet away from me.

I build a scale-model of our home out of Legos, showing two-year-old Julien how we had prepared for the storm: how we had boarded up the vulnerable back window, and how the wind would slam into the house and might whip around the next-door palm tree when the hurricane hit. We play out various scenarios, and Julien grunts his affirmative "Hmph!" with each demonstration. At that scale, it seems manageable.

Overnight the winds pick up, rattling our old windows, and the air starts to change. At three in the morning, I get up and pack the car; at 4:00 a.m. we drive off, Julien slumbering in the back seat. We don't necessarily know anything more about the storm at that point—it is still "trying to become better organized"—but it is time for us to go.

The roads are empty as we drive out of the city on US-10. We have slipped onto the road between the initial and final waves of evacuations. As we merge onto the highway we see the first droplets of rain on the windshield.

We can practically feel the heavy penumbra of sherbet spreading over the city—and what a peculiar feeling to be speeding away from it, sitting in a reclined chair in a somewhat aerodynamic 2700-lb metal box on wheels. During those predawn hours I keep looking back in the rearview mirror at the glowing cloud mass. How big is it? Is it building? How bad will it get? What about our house? Have we made the right choice? Should we be there with our friends who stayed? All these questions and more are at turns enhanced and subsumed by the necessary myopia that is driving away.

Later in the morning as we zoom up I-55 we see shattered turtle shells, the leftovers of ruined would-be highway crossers, and shredded armadillos balled up on the side of the road. And of course, there are the ubiquitous black forms of ejected truck tire husks, sometimes dangerously curling up in and between the lanes. There's something singularly terrifying about watching a big-rig shed a tire in real time, everyone speeding along merrily at eighty miles per hour while a certain tire that only *you* can see starts to buckle, flap on its wheel, and begin to disintegrate, leaving its carnage to flip and tumble behind, for other cars to veer around or run over.

Then there are billboards advertising hamburger choices, and others lambasting abortion—and still more billboards selling billboard space itself, a veritable landscape of meta-advertising.

*   *   *

The hurricane has passed over, knocking out power and blowing roofs off houses. We are spending a few days in St.

Louis, where Julien is getting some unexpected quality time with his grandparents. It is good to see him running around the big backyard and making up games in this new place.

But I miss our home. In my mind I keep trying to mentally inhabit it—to check a certain leak in the ceiling, to mop up the drips around the fireplace, or to stand over that one crack in the floorboards where the wind always whistles in underfoot. I find myself imagining what the house is feeling as the storm moves through. The house is old, and this is one of many, many storms it has been through—it probably has its own patterns and flexions for dealing with such torrents of wind and rain. I imagine the whine of generators interspersed around our neighborhood.

On our way north on I-55, we passed several dozen energy company bucket trucks that were headed south, driving in teams, toward the Gulf Coast. Help on its way.

*   *   *

We make it home after a long drive back, full of anticipation and uncertainty, wondering how our home has weathered the storm and hoping everything is (at least mostly) all right. The last hour of the drive is stunningly beautiful, cruising over the bloated wetlands as the clouds build and tumble in the distance. Beautiful, of course, with a post-sublime sort of caveat.

Rolling back into town I am struck by the bent road signs, ripped-up billboards, and piles of debris in the neutral ground. The lights at intersections are either blinking red and yellow or altogether dark—cars chaotically stopping and going, traffic somehow moving along. People amble down the streets in what looks like a semi-daze. Utility trucks can be seen in every direction, cherry pickers raised and men with fire-proof gauntlets hard at work, the balmy afternoon temperature ninety-five degrees.

I have been thinking about how the smells of New Orleans seep up from the ground. I experience this in a whole new way on returning, after Hurricane Isaac slowly organized, sat and spun for a while over the city, and finally blew through.

The garbage around town hasn't been picked up for days, in some cases a week, and to walk the blocks now is to rather swim through fetid scent clouds of slimy plastic wrappers; collapsed cardboard boxes; dead rats and mice that crawled into the garbage cans and could not get back out; stale beer, orange juice, milk, and liquid X; bulging diapers; decaying chicken wings and ham bones and ribs and shrimp heads; moldy bread; waterlogged fiberboard; vertically packed oak leaves layered in tessellating, gorgeous designs . . . to name a mere few of the recognizable objects festering on the street post-hurricane.

Our small house has made it through okay, no major damage on the outside. A gnarly old crepe myrtle tree in front of our home was snapped off at the base of its trunk and is now lying in the street right where our car would have been parked, had we stayed. And part of our front room ceiling is ballooning with rainwater, cracking in some places.

I had left a plastic storage bin beneath this spot before we left town (it dripped a little during the last tropical storm), and I'm glad I did: there are about four gallons of yellowish water in it. The house has a stale smell now, wafting down from the cracks in the ceiling. I need to crawl up to that point in our attic to check it out, but I'm procrastinating—it's not going to be pretty. I know we'll probably have to have significant work done on that part of the roof, termites are attracted to it, and so on—but we want to put a metal roof on the whole house, which is going to be a major endeavor, so I'm delaying for now.

And anyway I'm busy getting back to things, trying to reclaim something like everyday life. But it's hard to shake a hurricane, even when you've dodged the worst of it. Evacuating hurricanes becomes a cyclical adventure, a familiar collection of actions, contingencies, and risks. But it is no less scary each time the possibility of evacuation looms. And loom more and more, it does.

*   *   *

Night sounds of New Orleans: steel beams clanging near the river, elaborate songs of mockingbirds, helicopters chopping sticky air, cockroaches flying around a dark house, local freight trains, the Times Pic delivery car with wonky wheel.

*   *   *

The F16s that regularly tear open the sky over my home in New Orleans: they frighten me, but they also demand attention. What are those adventures, the ones we practice for but would never want to see realized?

*   *   *

2013: The sound of a grocery cart trundling down the street at 3:48 in the morning. I leave the house at 5:45 a.m. and walk twenty minutes to the Mississippi River. By first light I am standing in the current up to my knees on a sandy shelf of submerged willow saplings, their leaves and other things, from ribbons of Rite-Aid shopping bags to torn sweatshirt sleeves, swirling around my legs and feet.

I'm here to fly-fish. Fish are exploding all over the surface of the water, some of them rocketing six-feet high, repeatedly shooting out and slapping back in (they don't change angles enough to actually "dive" back in—mullet). Some of the fish look more like monsters, enormous scaly backs breaching the surface. The lights from the warehouses and docks across the river cast eerie reflections on the smooth water. I catch a few small ladyfish and a white bass. (A couple of days later, I hear someone at the fly shop describe ladyfish as "poor man's tarpon." I also learn that their family name *elopidae* comes from the Greek *ellops*, for a kind of serpent. And they do have a silvery serpentine quality, especially when they are schooling, as they seemed to be that morning.)

But catching fish is really only a small part of this adventure, an excuse or justification to stand in this place and notice other things—like seeing the dawn clouds stack up across the river, and exploring the weird riparian ecosystem under dense willow canopies. Someone has left a shrine of some sort in a willow stump, a carefully arranged (now burned down) candle, with attendant trinkets whose meaning and value are unknown to me. One of the things that arrests me as I fish is a hauntingly beautiful tinkling music fading in and out; upon investigation, I realize that it is the sound of broken glass from thousands of hurled beer bottles intermingling with myriad shells and stones washed up from the river, both of which gently collide with the wire retaining mesh holding up the riprap. The sound is barely audible, but mesmerizing once you hear it. A postmodern version of an Aeolian harp. Another sensation arrives with the silent approach of a giant crude oil tanker bearing the name Eagle Torrance, which glides by me heading upriver. After the ship passes, an enormous wake comes rolling in, really impressively huge waves that disturb the fish and send them scattering and jumping like crazy. The swells take me by surprise and I get wet up to my waist, but the disturbance is somehow delightful, changing the feel of the river suddenly and dramatically. I think of my student Stewart, who is working on a thesis project on surfing, and I wonder if anyone surfs the waves created by ship wakes on the river—the swells are really that big and strong, when they surge.

I owe this experience to a mystery person named Brian, whom I'd seen fly-fishing down here for a while. One day I finally worked up the nerve to climb down the riprap (cradling infant Julien) and chat with him; Brian turned out to be the nicest guy, and he intrigued me with his articulate knowledge of the river and his low-key approach to fly-fishing. I've always been like this myself, fishing as more of something that just comes naturally to me rather than treated as a high-tech, tricked-out form of sport or leisure. I have a couple of fishing shirts, but they are hardly recognizable as such. Anyway, Brian encouraged me to join him, and so, after spending the summer picking up my fly cast again in the lakes and beaver swamps of northern Michigan, I was ready to try it—and I'm so glad I did. I made it a regular thing. And the river is getting on *me*.

There's a Jim Harrison poem called "River VI," in which he alludes aptly to this feeling:

> The water slips around your foot like liquid time
> and you can't dry it off after its passage.

I'm getting used to—and used to looking forward to, but not being able to control—the small adventures that await me each time I go to the river. Surprises such as the perfect butternut squashes the other morning that were scattered along the bank, having fallen off some boat en route from Honduras. Then there was the alligator yesterday morning, just hanging out about twenty feet from the bank. Always these odd juxtapositions, the random and slightly ominous, here.

2014: One of those mornings in New Orleans where the thick smell of oil refining lays over the town and seeps through windows, floors, and walls. Buzzing electrical lines, sticky air, honey light, mockingbird taunts, skittering anole lizards, cloud-muffled 737s. One of those weird steamy days when you can actually feel New Orleans sinking into the gulf. When a closet door starts to stick and you realize it's not the frame or slider but rather that your whole house is slowly sinking. Street archaeology in New Orleans: asphalt, asphalt, cement, bricks, dirt. Camille is born. Our small house shrinks but manages to hold more adventures and love than ever before.

2015: New Orleans: where potholes bespeak the sea. Our backyard, such as it is, is a 15′-by-20′ concrete slab of paradise. The kumquats are shaping up nicely this year. You know you are raising a child in New Orleans when they say, "Look what I built out of Legos!"—and it's a highly detailed bar. Ian Bogost and I launch the Object Lessons book series, an elaborate publishing project that will change the way I teach, write, and exist as an academic. Julien starts to constantly identify things we should have books about: towels, cheese graters, alligators, bricks, sand, hurricanes. The objects we live with, each one an adventure to live with, to think with.

2016: The palmetto bugs in New Orleans are basically harmless. But sometimes in the middle of the night they'll startle you with their aura: they can command presence, fully inhabit your house. Boil water advisories: these adventures in hydration and contamination are not fun, and they sometimes stretch out for a day or more. Always having a few gallons of water in the cupboard, just in case. We get an estimate to build a "camelback" addition on top of our house, to fit our growing family—but it is astronomical (the estimate alone cleans out our savings account). We can't afford to live Uptown much longer.

2017: On a bright spring morning we leave our house at around eight o'clock, climb on our bicycles, and head from Uptown 7 miles downriver to join our friends for a parade. The ominously predicted rainstorms have held off, and the sky clears to unveil a beautiful day as we ride down a quiet one-way street toward downtown. We steer around strings of sparkling beads and sudden potholes, and hear occasional blasts of tubas and bass drums emanating over the neighborhoods. It is Mardi Gras.

Along the way we exchange friendly shouts of "Happy Mardi Gras!" and "All right, all right!" with random people sitting on their stoops or porches. After one such exchange Camille asks, "Is that your friend?" And I respond with something like, "When you're on a bike, everyone is your friend."

I wasn't really thinking about it at the time, but over the course of the day this strikes me as increasingly true: bicycling is a fundamentally different way of inhabiting this urban space. We are thrilled to see the new Blue Bike stations scattered around downtown, and even happier to see people riding these rental bikes throughout the day. This urban bicycling thing is taking off here, it seems. After a year of gloomy news, this is somehow a moving sign of hope.

We pass a pay-to-park lot near the French Quarter, and the attendant with a PARK sign waves at us and calls out, "You've got the best ride in the city!" Approaching our friends' home in the Bywater, a couple of cyclists with a flat tire flag us down;

we dismount and help them pump it back up. At our friends' place we lock up our bikes and join the parade, chatting with friends and relishing the elaborate costumes, homemade floats, and a cacophony of music in waves.

*   *   *

The Platonic form of an urban bicycle commute is this: crisp morning air in the lungs, a sleek frame and thin tires, panniers tight behind the saddle, legs pumping as the cyclist coasts through a bike lane, past cars and trucks, an elegant way to work.

My daily commute through the streets of New Orleans looks nothing like this. I am hauling my daughter to preschool in a cumbersome trailer, well aware that I am jeopardizing her life each time I push out onto the narrow streets, jockeying for position among Land Rovers, Safaris, and Dodge Rams. Their adventure is our possible demise. My ride is an old Specialized mountain bike I converted into a single-speed for urban use; it has a lightweight aluminum frame that is as punishing on the streets here as it used to be forgiving in the mountains and deserts where I first rode it new seventeen years prior.

New Orleans is mostly flat and there are plenty of one-way streets, so it's fairly easy to get around, compared to many cities. But that doesn't mean that drivers understand sharing the roads, or that the roads don't sometimes disintegrate into postapocalyptic rubble fields or other concrete aporia.

Bicycling in New Orleans is a synesthetic experience, in which drivers angrily honk and glare at me, wondering what *I* am doing on the road, even as I hug the curb. The thick scent of benzene regularly fills my nose as I ride—an unshakable reminder of oil extraction and refinement in the Gulf not so far away, and the environmental racism accreted around this industry. Sometimes we end up behind a garbage truck, awash in the fragrant detritus of the city for a block or so until we leave it behind. I dodge gaping sinkholes, watching them grow each day, edges falling off into the void—evidence of the subterraneous suck of coastal erosion. You can't deny ecological dynamism when on a bicycle saddle.

Still, even in the midst of all this, my daily rides can have a kind of strange beauty and even serenity.

During tropical storms or just after ordinary thundershowers, the dips in the streets will fill with water, sometimes up to six inches or even a foot. The city is mostly below sea level, and not by any accident. What was a passable block one day becomes a duck pond the next, with actual waterfowl scooting around, munching on . . . who knows what castoff morsels. We circumvent these spontaneous swamps, seeking minimally high ground. "The sliver by the river" is what they call the modicum of above-sea level land that abuts the Mississippi, our neighborhood.

Occasionally when we have ten minutes to spare, Camille and I take a longer route to her preschool, riding along the river at the southern end of Audubon Park. We watch the tugboats churning and pelicans cruising just above, wingtips sometimes grazing the surface as they soar by.

After I drop off Camille, I pedal down St. Charles to my campus a half-mile away, enjoying the thrill of riding alongside the streetcar as it rumbles by, passengers gazing out the open windows at the live oaks festooned with ferns and Spanish moss. No matter what was stressing me out the night before, or what deadline was hovering over me, my ride tunes me into myriad things and I feel a sensitized connection to this place by the time I arrive at work.

*   *   *

On the way back home after the St. Anne parade, our kids slumped and tired in the trailer, someone offers us to "pop a cap" with them—holding out a see-through plastic water pistol filled with whiskey. You shoot it into your mouth: a bizarre suicidal fantasy act turned inside out. We pass other cyclists weaving their way home after parades. Tourists often note that people in New Orleans are incredibly friendly and will just chat with you in the streets, and you notice this even more when on bike.

We are extra mindful of discarded beads this year, having learned of the forty-six tons of beads recently found to have clogged catch basins throughout the city, and not exactly helping the flooding situation. We have a few grocery bags full of beads that we've gathered off the streets near our house—for proper disposal if there is such a thing, but I'm not sure there is.

As we near our part of town, we glance down a side road and notice a flash of brightness: we've stumbled upon an elusive Mardi Gras Indian tribe, and we amble alongside them for a block as they turn onto Tchoupitoulas and continue their march.

All day I see frustrated drivers try to force their way through crowds and around meandering revelers. It takes us well over an hour to make our way from one side of the city to the other, and another hour or so to get home. The slowness is part of the beauty of the day.

This is Mardi Gras, a bizarre and special day in this one city on the "minor outlying island" (as the information forms allow us to rightly call it) that is New Orleans. But I can't help but think about the lessons to be taken away from this day and our cycling adventure. These are things I think about regularly when I ride, but which the carnival holiday brings into clear focus.

Bicycling is no mere pastime or hobby and is much more than an alternative means of transit. To get on a bike and ride through a city is a radically other mode of occupying the urban grid, and with it comes forms of openness and attention that are necessarily closed off by the confines of automobiles, no matter how cool they feel or how pricey they are. Elon Musk may have sent a fancy red sports car up into space as payload on his impressive endeavor the Falcon Heavy, in a symbolic gesture of human achievement. But it might have been more compelling, if less obvious, to have sent a bicycle up into the unknown, instead—because *that* is the way to be truly open to the unknown, including the unknown of the everyday all around.

2018: Side benefit of writing outside in New Orleans as the autumn mornings get cooler, and breezy: the occasional waft of roasting garlic coming from somewhere good. Julien puts it another way: "Papa, I like the smell of New Orleans. It's sort of sweet oily." We sell our small shotgun home in Uptown and buy a new house in Mid-City, four miles across town. The new house turns out to be part of a project designed by local architect Lee Ledbetter, whose work we have long admired when we visit the sculpture garden at the New Orleans Art Museum.

2019: A most unsettling sight today, spotted on my walk to pick up the kids from school: an LG flatscreen in a pile of banana palm leaves. On Mother's Day it starts raining at around 4:30 in the morning, a downpour. The flood quickly fills up the street in front of our house. Trash cans float down an urban river, white bags tumbling out and spreading. All the cars on the street are filled and totaled. The water reaches up to our third step before pausing, then recedes slowly. A three-foot-diameter whirlpool forms in the middle of the street as the catch basins finally start to suck the water out. Later we learn that the local pump house was not operational. Another hour of rain and our house would have flooded, too.

Vera is born a couple of weeks after the flash flood.

2020: Julien makes a New Year's resolution: he wants to learn to ride a bicycle by summer break. It is a great idea! But only an idea. I am not sure where we'll fit bikes into our budget (one for Julien and another for Camille, of course), though we do live near the greenway and could use it to practice safely, if indeed we find bikes.

We scuttle any active plans for this, keeping bicycling on the proverbial backburner, and start doing all the normal beginning-of-year things: back to school for the kids, mid-winter house cleaning, a new semester at my university . . . the grind. But with bright spots.

There are six monarch caterpillars on the milkweed plant in our backyard. The caterpillars have completely devoured the milkweed leaves and are now beginning to range around the yard, looking for more milkweed plants. But there aren't any more in our yard! Will they die? Or crawl to others elsewhere? We check on them every fifteen minutes, see where they are exploring. Could they make chrysalises now, here? By sheer coincidence, our friend Lizz happens to bring over a little milkweed plant as a gift. The caterpillars are happily chomping again. Small adventures.

*   *   *

I take a walk down the Lafitte Greenway to the new footbridge that passes over a bioswale. Insects whir in the undergrowth, and mockingbirds swoop in and out of the saplings. It's a magical spot in the middle of our city.

Walking by the canal a couple of blocks from my home, Camille and I watch a white heron stalk then catch and devour a surprisingly big fish. So there are fish in there. . . .

Then in February, we start hearing more and more about the novel coronavirus. By March, cases are popping up all over the city. I teach my last class outside one afternoon, right before the announcement that we were going online. The class feels a bit like the closing moments of *Melancholia.*

After all the schools go remote, but before the lockdowns go into effect, we pack our car and head north to the woods of Michigan. The roads are quiet and the usual touristy spots are desolate; no one is around. And they are not allowed to come. Seeing a rare opening, we jump at the chance: maybe the kids can learn to ride bikes, after all.

My generous mother-in-law manages to buy bicycles for Julien and Camille online before they all but disappear from the market, thanks to interruptions in the supply chain. I find them helmets, and on a cool but sunny April morning, we walk the bikes to a nearby church parking lot (empty). They throw their legs over the frames, push themselves onto their seats, and balance and fall . . . pedal and fall, pedal a bit longer, wobble—and fall. They keep falling, and keep getting up and trying again. Camille gets the hang of it first, racing circles around Julien and bragging. Then she tumbles and really scrapes her leg this time, and is humbled. But keeps at it.

I look at a video I took of Julien when he first stayed on, and I can hear his scared panting as his knobby knees pump to keep forward momentum. In the last moment of the video, the handlebars turn too far and he plummets to the ground—the video ends right before he hits the ground, a look of terror on his frozen face. (In the next video, though, he's grinning.)

Within a couple of days they are riding together, a miniature bike gang of two, razzing each other but pedaling together and gaining confidence with each ride. At a certain point, Julien pauses and realizes something: "I fulfilled my New Year's resolution!"

*   *   *

It is still the early months of what will become a wretched, drawn-out year of illnesses, deaths, paranoia, fanaticism, and heightened awareness of public health. Looking back now, I see that those weeks when my kids learned to ride bicycles were a rare bright spot of 2020.

Seeing their faces as they zip along a trail through the woods, watching them fall and pick themselves back up again, gradually mastering this quiet form of transit—it all gives me hope, even now as I revisit this memory from almost three years on.

We might get through this time, find ourselves in a better place. And not just the "same" place, the normal pre-pandemic hustle. No, watching my kids learn to ride gives me a different kind of hope: a hope for younger generations to not just rebound from the ecological catastrophes and economic structures based on inequity but to change their material conditions for the better. This is the adventure they have before them—one that embraces limits.

I hadn't thought that watching my kids learn to ride bikes would have such a profound impact on me. I knew it would be difficult, an investment of some time and lots of bruises and skinned knees. Plenty of encouragement, along the way.

But I never anticipated the rush of emotion and hope that would come from seeing them ride away from me, steadying themselves, discovering that new forms of mobility, of living, are still possible.

*   *   *

Back in New Orleans after the long quarantine spring and summer. Nearly every morning of the school year I take a two-mile walk: down the Lafitte Greenway, in Mid-City New Orleans, to I-10 and back home. The Old Basin Canal runs along the Greenway, but is mostly invisible—buried as it is well below streets, parking lots, and meandering drainage systems. Completed in 1796, this corridor connected Bayou St. John (which flows off Lake Pontchartrain) to the edge of the French Quarter, two miles away. During the decades after it was built, the canal was a main commercial throughway for goods coming to the city from the West. The canal was gradually supplanted by other avenues into the city and was almost entirely filled and covered over in 1938.

Where the water is still briefly visible, it is a concrete channel near my home that somedays runs gin clear, and other days resembles Kahlua. There's one part where an exposed passage siphons and drops six inches, and when the current is pushing hard enough there's a standing wave that I can hear from up above. It reminds me of a certain wave I camped next to in the Grand Canyon many years ago: it looks like Hermit Rapids, only smaller. Plastic bottle caps shoot the rapids, adventures in miniature. But for the most part, the canal is a slow if steady stream of water running over old mattress springs, bicycle frames, undulating shredded shirts, and discarded beer bottles. For a couple of weeks last fall there was a teal velvet sofa sitting at the edge of the canal wall; each morning it would be at a different angle, with new stains. One morning it was gone.

I start paying attention to what is down in the canal: sometimes a bittern, other times a white heron, and once a feral black cat. There are fish in the water, too: tiny darters, mostly, but also what I recognize as Rio Grande cichlids—

aquarium fish that got loose after a hurricane and which took over a lot of the waterways around town. When the fish are spawning, they have a distinctive, almost festive two-tone appearance: white heads, and darker bodies. According to the fish and wildlife service, if you catch a Rio Grande you are not supposed to release it back into the water. You're supposed to "destroy" it. These cichlids are related to tilapia, farmed fish which are widely available and often prepared and served at restaurants.

Another morning I notice that someone has dangled a milk crate in the canal near the pump station on Broad, either to catch fish or maybe to feed the large turtle that I sometimes see. But it's also possible that the milk crate on a string could just be elaborate litter. There is so much garbage in the canal; it regenerates each morning.

The water runs gracefully across tossed-off high-tops, old bed frames, and vandalized road signs and parking meters alike. But there are also blooms of aquatic vegetation, vivid green corridors and cubbies that I increasingly notice the fish moving through. I start to watch schools of small bream shooting around in eddies near the canal walls.

One time as I walk up to the canal I am startled to see the current churning in the *opposite* direction—as if the world had suddenly been flipped upside down, or turned on its axis the wrong way. The nearby pump must have been reversed, for some inscrutable maintenance reason. (In fact, as I would later find out from a local engineer, this was the cause of a pump malfunction, when the sheer power of gravity turns things around and makes the water move the way it's not supposed to—at least according to us.) It bends the brain when you see water running in a way you're not expecting. It is confounding, and I wonder how the fish are dealing with this bizarre inversion, their weed beds being pulled all askew and backward.

For a few days there is what looks like a black Ikea Billy bookcase lodged between an old wheel and the wall; the fish duck in and out of the swollen particleboard refuge. I start to notice larger fish, in the six-inch range, moving in and out of its rectilinear shadows. With every storm, as the water level rises, then subsides again, stuff gets washed away, and new structure appears for the fish. The Billy is swept off into oblivion, but other furniture crops up, only later to disappear, too.

I watch the cichlids make circular indentations for spawning, and then aggressively protect the beds from other fishes' intrusions. Life and nonlife, waste and fecundity commingle here.

*   *   *

I kept my sanity during the spring and summer of 2020 by fly-fishing nearly every day while we were up in Michigan. The national lakeshore near my home up there was closed—except for those who could walk in, so I was usually alone on the water—well, "alone" other than the millions of fishes and frogs and snapping turtles and snakes and birds and insects and larvae and plants and . . . everything else. Plus, curious beavers swimming up to me, deer sneaking through the woods, and coyotes loping on the shoreline . . . . Alone, that is, but not at all. During those intense months early in the pandemic, being among these myriad creatures kept me grounded—if in water, too.

Now back in New Orleans, back in our workaday routines, and Covid-19 notwithstanding, I need to fish again. So I take my simple seven-foot Tenkara rod and some small nymph-pattern flies to the canal one morning. I always wanted to catch a Rio Grande cichlid.

The first time I cast my line into the water, I don't attract anything. Or, I might catch momentary interest from a fish, carefully twitching my fly around a cinder block, but then the fish will veer off in disgust. They are smart. I drop my fly next to a patch of submerged jungle and navigate it around a floating blue face mask. Masks have become a new kind of lily pad in the canal. Still, nothing. Maybe I am not using the right fly.

I go home and get out my fly-tying vise and materials, and scour the internet for "flies for cichlids." I tie some very small admixtures of minnow patterns and injured insects. I incorporate fluorescent orange marabou and dashes of chartreuse crystal flash. I tie modified nymphs with brass bead-heads and electric blue puffy bodies. Anything to look toxic and delicious.

Most days I just watch the fish as I walk past, on my longer brief journeys. But next time it is overcast and the timing is right, I take my rod and line and box of flies and try again. This time, I catch fish.

I don't catch a cichlid, but I do catch something even more special: a green sunfish, *Lepomis cyanellus*, a wily species of fish that I caught a lot when I was around eleven, at the time when I first learned to fish. This fish sends me on a water slide ride through my mind, and suddenly there I am back standing on the grass next to a small farm pond in Okemos, Michigan, catching the same fish.

In the canal I also catch a largemouth bass—which surprises me, as they are typically found in larger waters. I snap photos of these two fish and send them to my fishing buddy Glen, up in Michigan. He replies, "I can't believe how healthy they look, coming out of *that* water!" It is true. Both fish bear beautiful markings and are picture-perfect—little gems in the midst of the urban filth and flowing waste. I release both of these fish back into the canal. I am thrilled by the relative diversity of species in this miniscule urban wash near my home.

I keep monitoring these fish in the dynamic lifeworld of the canal, as our pandemic fall drags on. The cichlids prove elusive to catch. I start to plan a smaller, intricately textured fly in my head: I'll call it the Carondelet Crawler.

Each day reveals new graffiti on the pump house, new trash bags amassed or spewing open on the street, herons and crows roving the channel. On my walks, I mentally construct my new fly: a tiny black marabou tail, some peacock herl with two strands of red crystal flash up front, six rubber legs . . . .

Then Hurricane Zeta appears in the gulf. It organizes rapidly and heads (maybe) toward us. I stockpile water and food, tie everything down that might blow away . . . then watch the storm come churning directly over our house. We experience the eerie peach glow of the eye of the storm pass overhead, right around sundown.

Power is out; tree limbs are down all over town. Tying flies and catching fish are the furthest things from my mind.

*   *   *

When we finally venture out of our home, we are hit with the thick aroma of diesel fuel. The air is dense with fumes; we can hardly breathe on our back porch. *What the fuck?*

After we clean up and find our bearings, I go on my usual morning walk. As I round the corner to the greenway, I see a bunch of pump trucks parked alongside the canal. The smell is stronger than ever. When I look down into the water—well, it *isn't* water. The channel is covered with a slick film, milky orange rainbows undulating sluggishly, blooming spectrums all wrong. This is the fuel we are smelling, even from a couple of blocks away.

I ask one of the workers who is manipulating one of the big tubes, sucking off the top layer into a giant cylinder on a trailer parked next to the canal, what is going on. "Some kind of spill. Maybe from the pump house." He cocks his head toward the massive green tubes that seem to lurch out of the ground and into the pump house across the street.

The truck attached to the trailer says something like Environmental Solutions. Or maybe it is Environmental Strategies. The word "Management" might be involved. I can't quite focus, for the stench. Down in the water, I see a dead fish; I could swear it is the same green sunfish I caught and released a few weeks earlier. The vegetation is wilted and scorched, where it used to reach vibrantly above the surface. Styrofoam cups and plastic detritus gather in the nylon catch ropes that are stretched across the water.

I keep walking the Old Basin Canal, watching the spill keep spilling, day after day. The smell of fuel lingers, even as the water gradually clears. Various vehicles are parked adjacent to the canal for over a week, all bearing different geometric icons and official if imprecise sounding slogans on their doors and on the vast tank trailers. They remind me of the ominous cleanup crew that arrives at the landing site of the spaceship in *E.T.* Slapdash concoctions are slung over the water, ad hoc capturing assemblages somewhere between barriers and sponges. It all looks so thrown together, but then, who could plan for such a site-specific disaster?

On and on, fuel belches from the tunnel beneath Broad. One day I see a grimy johnboat and a pirogue on the sidewalk, apparently having just finished with a hands-on venture down *in* the canal. Another day I chat with three Louisiana fish and wildlife workers standing in front of a black pickup, who are surveying the scene and jotting things down in little notebooks. I tell them about the dead fish, the turtle, and the various species I'd spotted over the previous months. They write it all down. They seem incredulous that the canal had been home to such an array of life.

The stench from the fuel remains, the water below an oily mélange. I track down a tweet by our mayor that features a photo of the cleanup, vaguely describing a "diesel spillage"— and suggesting it was caused by citizens who had poured generator fuel into the drain during the storm. I reply to the mayor's tweet with a picture of the canal a week later, with the sheen of gas still prominent on the surface, asking *what happened here?*

A local engineer replies to me with a screen capture of a U.S. Coast Guard incident report grid, highlighting this line: "CALLER REPORTED A DIESEL TANK OVERFLOWED DUE TO HURRICANE ZETA, SOME WHICH GOT INTO A STORM DRAIN." The address of the spill is listed as 3000 Perdido Street: the county jail, a mile away from the canal. What does the prison industrial complex have to do with this tragedy? Apparently, the diesel is flowing from a catch basin near the jail in our direction and emerging here in the canal. But it is a lot more than "some" fuel. And "into a storm drain"—as if it just goes away, then? Storm drains always go somewhere else—and usually toward where poorer and disadvantaged people live. And it being "due" to the hurricane—as in, strong wind blew over a tank? I try to discover more details, but the city's infrastructural problems are manifold, and amid the post-storm cleanup this one "incident" fades quickly into the remote past of social media outcry. Rainbow plumes remain visible in the water over the following months.

It eventually clears, but the life is gone. I don't see any fish in the water—no more turtles, either. White herons still hunt anoles in the willows off the Greenway, above . . . but I don't see them stalking fish in the canal. I finally see a pair of mallards making their way at a ferry angle across the tepid current, but they seem disoriented, unsure of where they are. Maybe last year at this time, the canal was their honey hole.

*　*　*

The water continues to pump through the canal, from the myriad drains across town into Bayou St. John and out, eventually, into Lake Pontchartrain and out into the Gulf of Mexico. I had become attached to this lively ecosystem rife with plump fish improbably living amid the disgusting refuse of Mid-City. Now it is all but a dead zone. And there are no repercussions or sustained remediation, after the baroque cleanup efforts that wrap up as unceremoniously as they began. For a few weeks following the spill, I watch the local news sites and search for keywords online to see if anyone is investigating the spill, or if there is any follow-up reporting. But nothing ever appears.

I want to find out exactly what had happened here, to make people aware of the disaster. Of course, this is happening in late 2020, and tragedies are already piled to the ceilings of hospitals and morgues, not to mention clogging everyone's minds. What is a polluted waterway and some dead fish, in the final analysis? As I approach the canal one morning in late

November, a statuesque black-crested night heron perches on one of the concrete beams, staring resolutely down into the water, as if willing fish to reappear—knowing they should be there.

The graffiti on the pump house is painted over, then appears again, different tags and slogans. A scrawl on the wall one morning says, "Save the future!" I keep walking by the canal each morning, looking down into the water for fish, monitoring the confused pair of ducks, and looking for other signs of life. And bracing for the next incident, another indiscriminate dump into the storm drain—or worse.

2021: Back to school. Coming out of the pandemic, haltingly. Then tropical Storm Ida forms in the Gulf of Mexico and is predicted to make landfall as a category 4 hurricane the following morning. Time to finish preparations. The line at the gas station is several dozen cars deep, by the time I arrive at a sensible 8:10, after dropping my kids off at school. I gamble, and decide to go back later. (Not a great decision, in hindsight.)

We've done this many times now—enough that I've lost track over the years, storms that we've frantically prepared for, and sometimes fled. Now we brace for the latest hurricane to arrive. They're already calling this one "catastrophic," even as it departs Cuba and heads north over the Gulf of Mexico, still twenty-four hours away from us.

For many, climate change is a remote reality, or something of a long game; for those who don't believe in climate change, it's even a *non*-game—or just a fiction, an unreality. But for those of us who live on the Gulf Coast (and in other coastal regions and threatened environments), climate change is all too real, its effects increasingly encroaching. There is no denying the rising temperatures of the Gulf of Mexico that foment more frequent and stronger storms with each passing year. It's not a game at all.

What's hard to explain is how contorted and stuttered the actual process of hurricane preparation can be, as well as the decisions and stressors that pop up along the way. Yet it's also mundane. At the first hints of a tropical storm that might form into a hurricane, locals start watching the "cone of uncertainty" take shape. Will it hit us? Veer one way or another? Stall out over the gulf? Even if there's a *chance* of impact, the stockpiling and preparations begin.

I head to the grocery store to get gallon jugs of water (almost cleared out, already), and charcoal and food for grilling in case we lose power. And plenty of sundries that require no heating up at all. A single can of Amy's low-sodium refried beans lies on its side on the shelf—you always find out which consumer items are the least popular, before a hurricane. I figure I might as well get batteries for flashlights, even though last year's are somewhere in the house already, badgered away for *that* hurricane, or more likely redeployed into various children's toys, half spent.

There is no special support fund for these last-minute expenses. You either put them on your credit card or plunder any savings you might have, to get ready for a storm. And when hurricane prep must be done multiple times in one season, the financial burden adds up quickly.

Evacuation is always a possibility, too—but the calculus around evacuating is nebulous and shifty. If and when to go are matters that are guided as much by personal necessity and caution as they are dictated by central mandates and weather reports. And then, there are really only a few routes out of New Orleans (this city is technically an island). It's hard to describe the strange suspense and uncertainty that builds in the mind as you anxiously watch a hurricane's development on websites and weather-tracking apps, and plot a possible escape. When is it too late? What's the cutoff time? Which way to go? Often, the minutes and hours of indecision take place through the night, wrecking sleep on top of everything else. Of course, many people don't have any choice but to "shelter in place," as the saying goes.

For those whose houses or businesses are at ground level, sandbags become necessary. Yes: Many people have to resort to literal, hand-filled *bags of sand* to keep floodwater from inundating homes or shops. Also, we tie down everything that could get turned into a projectile by gale force winds: outside chairs, tables, the grill, kids' playthings . . . it all has to get strapped down or secured to something (a porch, a fence), or put away in a closet or shed.

These are some of the low-tech tactical realities of hurricane preparation. For every dramatic flight of a Hurricane Hunter or abstract digital rendering of the storm's path, there are also countless quotidian acts on the ground of ordinary humans getting ready, once again, to be pummeled by very real effects of climate change. It's a cycle, but one that is getting exacerbated each year. And while we may be the victims, we're also thoroughly implicated.

*   *   *

We are waiting for the storm. Long hours noticing the wind speeds increase gradually until the howl is nearly constant. Our willow in the backyard looks like it might take off and fly, like a flimsy frayed umbrella left open on the ground in a gale. We tuck Julien and Camille in for bed even as the sheets of rain pelt the windows right above their heads, the branches of the giant live oaks on the street just outside quaking and snapping, leaves snapping every which way. I check the satellite view of the storm to monitor its progress and check the energy company's outage map, watching as our friends all over town lose power, neighborhood by neighborhood, the crimson lines growing on the map and getting closer to us and closer still until sometime in the evening when everything goes dark, and silent, save for the wind and rain. We turn a white noise iPad app on for Vera, so she can keep sleeping through the storm and we can get at least eight hours out of it, and then we lie in bed and brace as each gust knocks the house. At around midnight, the wind finally begins to subside.

*   *   *

Against all odds, everyone wakes up at around their standard times. The hurricane has passed. The sunrise is brilliant, the air crisp and unusually fresh smelling. (The faint oil smell is not present, for once.)

Amazingly we still have water pressure, and our gas line is functioning. So we get up and I make a somewhat ordinary breakfast: a big skillet of hash browns (we had potatoes to use up) and scrambled eggs. I had ground coffee beans the day prior and pulled out our old Moka espresso pot to make thick rich coffee on the stove. Everyone fed, I venture outside to assess the block and take stock of the damage.

Live oak limbs and leaves cover the street in front of house, mixed together with debris from tipped dumpsters. A nearby auto shop must have blown open, because I notice the remnants of various tire-repair accouterments scattered all around.

I drag our garbage can and our next-door neighbors' can out to the curb and start loading them up with the detritus. So much biomass: greenery usually living over and above us, now decaying on the ground. Pounds and pounds and pounds of these intricately twisting branchlets and twigs. I am struck by how brittle the live oak branches are, as I scoop them up and smash them down in the garbage cans—how could these trees be so strong, too? These trees in front of our house have survived hurricanes for over a hundred years, mostly intact. Brittle but strong: there's a lesson here for adventure.

At one point in the morning a team of regional transit authority workers comes out to clear the road. There is one particularly big branch (the size of a Jeep) in the middle of the road that needed moving, and I help a worker drag it to the curb. I ask if he is okay, everything safe, and he says he lives in Lafitte and hasn't been home yet—that's where the waters were predicted to be the highest. He looks worried, if also resigned. I wish him luck and he thanks me and we both move on.

Our willow's entire shape has shifted several feet to the northwest—a visibly noticeable difference, like it's an entirely other tree now. Its roots are pulled up out from under the surface of the ground, but they appear to be still holding on tight. The tree will live, just in an altered state, post-storm. The rest of our backyard is windswept and disfigured, but otherwise okay. Three unripened Meyer lemons are scattered on the ground, but most of them have, incredibly, remained on the little tree (this is our first crop of them!).

Now sweating, I go back into the house. It is warming up inside. Julien and Camille are making comic books—a pastime they'd gotten into since having no internet up in Michigan—and Vera is busy playing with Duplos. From time to time Vera asks to talk to her grandparents on FaceTime, and we have to complicatedly explain the predicament at hand.

One of the unexpected pleasures of the day after the storm is the inoperability of our phones. No signal for most of the day . . . no way to use them, beyond as simple clocks.

Instead, I repose on the couch and finish Kim Stanley Robinson's *Red Mars*, which I'd been reading slowly since July. When was the last time I read a novel for a couple of hours straight, not once looking at my phone? It is otherworldly, in multiple senses. (Slight digression here: *Red Mars*, what an incredible novel! The literal world-building, the characters, the emplotment, the rendering of topography, the management of time and tension, the truly complex *adventure*! BUT, not the best book to be reading in anticipation of a major hurricane, or just after. One can only handle so much apocalypse and survival at once.)

Out in our backyard a little later, I look up and see terns wheeling in the sky, appearing ecstatic—though I'm quite sure that my impression is really just an anthropomorphic projection. Dragonflies, too, are zigging and zagging around; *clearly* they are energized and alive today, with or without me interpreting them as such.

Midmorning I take Vera for a walk around the block, and we notice the ravaged fences, terracotta roof tiles strewn about, plywood fragments, and one stretch of sidewalk festooned with hundreds of bloated diapers from the nearby daycare, whose trash cans had tipped and cascaded onto the street.

An odd thing about this whole experience is realizing the scalar discrepancies involved. From the outside, from the reports trickling in, it probably sounds and looks like an absolute horror show. And yes, it was a huge hurricane that barreled over the coast. But on the ground, it takes place at all these smaller scales: your house (even particular walls of your house, or parts of your yard); the block, pods of filth, and verdant ejecta; the adjoining roads; the neighborhood; the region—it's all impossible to map or track from a single perspective. You have to juggle multiple vantage points at once and somehow toggle mentally between them constantly, when you're living through it.

As if to prove this in another way, later in the day when we get a faint signal to our phones, an email from our kids' school blips through: "We just received notification that a student tested positive for COVID-19. If your child attended school on Thursday, August 26 OR Friday, August 27, your child is a close contact of this student."

Oh, right! A pandemic is still going on, while we've been preparing and living through a hurricane. No in-person school for our kids for a couple of weeks—as if there *would* be classes anyway now, all the public schools having closed "indefinitely," as we learned from another email update. In any case, it is an unsettling reminder of the *other* global emergency happening at this moment. What to do, now?!? Can we even leave town, knowing we might infect people along the way? Fortunately we had bought rapid tests from Walgreens some days before the storm, and we use them now to test. No positive results, yet, so we can maybe still evacuate in good conscience.

After cleaning up and emptying our warming fridge and freezer (so much good food, so little time to eat it before it spoils!), checking the block a few more times, we feel the temperature rising, as well as the ambient stress and panic around town. Time to go.

We pack up the car quickly and leave town in halting traffic, bound for . . . who knows? And who knows for how long. I write the bulk of these notes about the hurricane in a fleabag motel outside of Memphis, jotting them down on my phone as everyone falls asleep in the luxuriant waft of a whining wall-unit air conditioning system. We'll go on from here, watching the Entergy outage map, staying in touch with our neighbors—all checking in periodically on the block, on the city, on the state of things.

But what is this state of things, where we might have another storm next week—even a bigger storm? And the week after that, too? And next year, and the next? While matters of infrastructure improvements—not to mention actual, radical changes with respect to our entanglement with the ecosystem—seem removed and abstract to the point of being futile? It's dizzying to reconcile the ways we're stuck in the present—this static state called *progress*—with the encroaching realities of this planet, realities that are so much bigger than us, even if we've influenced them disproportionately.

My friend Tim Morton emails me a touching story today about their twelve-year-old son Simon, and the ways that Generation Z (and the next generation) are really the recipients of all this trouble—but also how they hold the potential for real change. This is a welcome note, as it grounds me in this groundless moment. It reminds me of what I'll go back for, what I *do*. My Ecological Thought seminar this semester suddenly seems all the more relevant, even if (or because!) we're in abeyance for the time being.

So once the power is restored we'll head back to New Orleans, to resettle in trepidation. To live in this state of growing uncertainty concerning the future, and what to make of it. Hardly the adventure we planned to have, but here we are.

* * *

Julien and I had been watching the Marvel "What If?" animated shows on Disney+ before the hurricane. Each episode plays out an alternative scenario with a main Marvel character that would distort and rearrange the sequence of events as we know them otherwise in the MCU. As we are watching the latest episode today—the first time I'd sat and zoned out since we started preparing for the storm—it occurs to me that there is something familiar about the setup of the series: it reminds me of mentally plotting out the possible domino effects and probable outcomes that we face as the storm got closer and finally swept over us.

It's fun to imagine different possible scenarios when it comes to fictional superhero characters and elaborate plot twists. It's not so much fun when it's just your normal life, and the contingencies are determined by the spaghetti models of a looming hurricane. Robinson Meyer writes eloquently at *The Atlantic* about the limits of hurricane preparation in the face of supercharged storms such as Ida. But while those seventy-four hours of bracing for the storm happened all too fast, the twelve hours of the *actual* storm slowed down and stretched out in weird ways. I am thinking back on the details of those distended minutes when we were *in* the storm, and here's what I remember:

First, there was the feel of the winds gradually increasing: it happens in fits and starts, each gust may be a new steady-high, or may be a fluke. But this happens over an excruciating duration, and you have to have external measuring devices to really gauge it across the hours. We have the willow tree in our backyard that we planted when we bought our house: it was the diameter of my thumb when I put it in the ground, a thin bare wand sticking out of the clayey soil, a few wispy branches suggesting *tree*. Now the trunk is as wide as my torso, and the foliage covers our whole fifteen- by twenty-foot yard. I watched the willow dance and undulate in the intensifying winds. By watching this tree, we could infer the steady uptick in wind speeds. (We were also watching a huge pecan tree getting rocked a few houses away, in the background; that is, we watched it until it was uprooted and came crashing to the ground, sending a plume of waxy green pinnately compound leaves up and away, and tearing through two fences along the way.)

Things flew by. Signs, shopping bags, blue face masks, plastic shrapnel, trashcan lids, branches, UFOs, more face masks, the rain itself in broad sheets—it was *almost* entertainment. When not looking outside, we were watching the utility company's outage map online: green lines turning red like some weird alien invasion game on the screen. Our lights flickered on and off throughout the afternoon, to the point that our internet service became useless. We switched to a hotspot, connecting to our phones; those Ozymandian cell towers would last, wouldn't they?

Improbably, we kept our electricity until around 5:30 in the evening—I snapped a screenshot of it toward the end, while we were feeling exceedingly lucky. Then the entire city blacked out. We had had our computers all charged for backup power for our phones, which were also plugged in up to the last instant. But all at once, it was just our little glowing phones in a dark house, and we quickly adjusted to *not* looking at them constantly. It was time to conserve power.

The eerie darkness of a city in total blackout is something to observe—not that you *want* to see that, in the midst of a hurricane. It's terrifying. But the sudden plunge into optical stillness—even in the middle of a hurricane!—is also remarkable, because you realize at once how numb you've become to panoramic splotches of light, glowing symbols, glaring WORDS, and other miscellaneous highly illuminated visual signals. Looking out back after the blackout, it was just a blue-gray landscape of oblique shapes and indistinct forms. It was somehow calming, even as the immediate meaning of the situation was that the storm had just dealt a definitive blow to the city and things would probably get worse. Maybe much worse.

This abruptly quiet monochromatic scene didn't last; we live near one of the main mass transit stations, and within minutes their emergency generators had kicked on, powering up their floodlights and adding a terrific roar to what was already a cacophony of sounds.

It's the persistent howling of the wind that is really unnerving. I grew up in Michigan and am used to winter blizzards and so-called "three day blows" that can dump feet of snow, or redistribute an entire coastline overnight. But those formative experiences didn't prepare me for the bell curve of twelve hours of hurricane winds, like a celestial super-villain slowly turning up the level on a planetary-scale fan and then just as incrementally turning it back down again. At its peak, a peak that lasted from about 8:00 p.m. to midnight, the wind was shaking our house so much that we really wondered if the windows, roof, and walls would hold—this is not a comfortable comportment to maintain for multiple hours.

We got our kids to sleep. Except for using little lanterns and flashlights, and ignoring the creaking walls and obscure thumps outside, it was almost ordinary. We read some books, cuddled, left them to sleep in their bedrooms that we secretly feared could get sheared from the front of the house. In retrospect, we probably should have huddled together downstairs, in a safer space of the house, all together. But Lara and I were already exhausted from the long day, and knowing it would be a drawn-out night with any number of disasters ahead, we selfishly opted for the easiest thing: keep to our routines, maybe get a few hours of quiet—house implosion be damned.

After a fitful few hours of slumber I woke up alert; it was almost one in the morning. The wind was definitely dying down. We had made it.

I looked outside at the murky urban skyline beneath racing clouds. Blackout. The hurricane had moved on; but now we were entering something else altogether.

*   *   *

It's been a little over two weeks since Hurricane Ida visited us. The streets are alive with the smell of garbage. Everyone's frozen and refrigerated food that couldn't be stored during the blackout is now rotting in bags in the sweltering heat. It's all there: erupting from black plastic trashcans. Piled against the curbs. Strewn about in the road. And now, it's getting soaked—and sometimes floating away. (The first bands of rain associated with Hurricane Nicholas are lashing the city, now.)

I walk through my neighborhood to Bayou St. John. The piles of garbage grow each day. Old broken microwaves, and boxes and packaging from new microwaves, litter the streets.

Sculptural miscellany, if belied by foul scents. With power back on and the city gradually coming back to life, it's not an acute problem—just a low-grade reminder of the dysfunction and chaos that lurks right under the surface, here. Wafts of death issue through alleys and across the fence in our backyard. Dead meat, dead plant matter, dead dinosaurs in the form of plastic, dead . . . cardboard, if that's possible?

While our house weathered the storm ok, our refrigerator was electrocuted after the power came back on. (I forgot to unplug it when we left town; a stupid, utterly avoidable mistake.) So we are living out of our freezer, which is bizarrely over-performing as if to make up for its in operable upstairs roommate, the fridge I think the actual meaning of this situation is that the fridge's evaporator fan is what shorted out, so the frozen air isn't circulating correctly . . . but after a storm, everything feels weirdly animate. Or dying, or dead.

*   *   *

2022: On the phone today with someone who is coming to New Orleans for the first time . . . they asked me what it was like, here . . . and I just thought about the Star Wars planet Bracca: masses and layers of familiar forms and technology, but everything broken or half-functioning.

Getting my kids their second shot this morning at their doctor's office, on the 7th floor. See all the blue tarps: roof damage from Ida. Every direction looks like this.

"Resilience" is a terribly overused word. To learn what resilience is, watch a milkweed plant get eaten bare, then watch it come back a couple of months later to feed the next generation of caterpillars. Resilience isn't just about bouncing back—it's about slow, improbable returning and regrowth.

*   *   *

On my morning walk, I spot a kingfisher cruising the canal— its drops and uplifts unmistakable.

*   *   *

Mark Yakich and I are having lunch at a taco place near campus. We spent the morning arranging a collection of Greg Keeler's poems, which we are preparing to send to another friend who runs a small press. It is hot. It's mid-August, and a band of strong thunderstorms has just swept across the city. The steam from evaporating puddles makes the day feel even hotter. As we sit under a canopy and pour water into our cups to drink, we smell something and hear it at the same time: a sewage pumping truck parked adjacent to the restaurant, wafts of human waste washing over us as the pumper pumps, a beleaguered whine. Our waitress saunters over and apologizes profusely, but Mark says since he just had Covid, he could barely smell anything anyway; and I say I just appreciate the irony of it all. Only in New Orleans: delicious food and moldering filth, in such close proximity. Relieved, our waitress laughs in agreement and says something that Mark and I linger on for several minutes: "Nowhere else!"

Mark once made a series of paintings called "The Mountains of New Orleans." They are comprised of blobs of colors that from a certain distance resemble landforms, topography, a horizon, sky. Of course, there are no mountains in New Orleans, unless the shifting spectacular clouds count. The mountains are in the mind, and formed by putting color fields next to one another. Mark has painted these over the years as a way to survive, a meditative practice. It's an adventure in making and seeing, inspired by nowhere else.

*　*　*

It takes me just under an hour to walk from my home in Mid-City to the university campus where I teach. If I can't bicycle to work, I like to walk it. Four miles, crossing over Highway 10 and meandering through a maze of neighborhoods and invariably circumnavigating torn-up roads and sidewalks, zones of perpetual closure and rerouting. I don't do it every day or even every week, but whenever I walk to work, it's an adventure in the fullest sense. An adventure that ripples out to the broader dimensions and textures of this tattered, pungent, beautiful, fraught city.

The first few blocks take me past the homes of Latin American families, many of whom work construction jobs around town. I hear my neighbors rev their pickups on the street in front of our house at just before 6:00 a.m. each morning, loading ladders and coolers and toolboxes into the beds of their trucks before they rumble off for the day toward building sites. This makes me remember the day that the under-construction Hard Rock Hotel, about a mile from our home, partially collapsed—injuring twenty construction workers and killing three, though some bodies were not recoverable, other corpses hung visibly from the wreckage, and the exact number of missing and dead seemed to shift around, a cloud of ambiguity not unlike the horrible dust cloud that followed the disaster.

A few weeks later, the whole damaged structure and precariously leaning cranes were demolished with a strategic demolition, the explosions of which we felt in our house before hearing them. An uncanny feeling lingered around that time. I wondered then about how much of the terror of the collapse, then the bizarre catharsis of the demolition, had to do with the city having escaped (at least *that* fall) another storm season, but with a couple of close calls. It can feel as if we are all bracing here for disaster of one sort or another, all the time. And in the summer time, this anticipation gets especially amped up, this bracing and waiting and preparing, and this year we were especially tweaked because of the flash floods of the prior spring and mid-summer, not to mention the multiple boil water advisories over the past year or so. Like we're just waiting to be wiped off the planet, or at least washed into the gulf. Then this hotel collapse happened, which was an awful if relatively contained disaster. And then, as if that wasn't enough, we had to concoct an insane spectacle of destruction around it, even to the point of turning into a spectator sport, an event, a "building toxic event," to adapt DeLillo's phrase from *White Noise*. It feels violent and hodgepodge and . . . ultimately incomplete and anticlimactic. As if we all know that the real climax is yet to come—and we can't control it, even if we're a pretty key part of its production.

My Tulane pal Tom Beller compared the demolition to 9/11, for the fixation the city had with it—intense, abject, grotesquely captivating. This was like our own desperate, self-inflicted, and pitiful version of that event: our elastic fifteen minutes of Warhol-esque fame, amounting in . . . I'm not sure what. We had a Hard Rock Hotel under construction, reaching for the sky; it partially collapsed; then we had to demolish it for safety reasons. There was one photo that the local news site posted that was particularly 9/11-ish: balls of flame ejecting from a built structure, the cranes acting as our spindly twin towers.

It felt like no coincidence, too, that the city's new airport was just about to have its grand opening. As the smoke and dust cleared and the rubble of the Hard Rock Hotel settled, I was making plans to drive to an open house to celebrate the pre-opening of the new airport—a story I told in my book *Grounded*.

But that was a tangent; I'm still walking past my neighbors' houses. I keep walking, down my street, noticing a dead rat, some feral cats, an abandoned leather Lay-Z-Boy recliner, and an old big-screen TV on the curb. There are still piles of trash and mounds of dirt and branches left over from Hurricane Ida cleanup—a year ago now. We still don't have recycling service restored in our neighborhood, a year later. Cans, bottles, and cardboard intermingle with clovers and cat claw vines.

Where my street meets the boulevard that was recently renamed Norman C. Francis (changed from Jefferson Davis), I turn to the left to head uptown. If I were to turn to the right, I would head toward the end of Bayou St. John, where I go a few times a week to fly-fish for an hour or so, to clear my head. When I spotted a *New York Times* photo essay, "Documenting Los Angeles's Unlikely Urban Fishermen," I could relate. The piece centers on a stretch of the Los Angeles River called the Glendale Narrows, where the author Madeline Tolle observes an assortment of people who fish in this gritty riparian ecosystem. Tolle concludes idyllically, describing the pursuit as "just a small respite, a break from the daily grind."

It's true; this is my daily respite, too. Recently I learned how to catch the elusive mullet that leap from the water charismatically, but who are vegetarian and so won't exactly pursue a typical "fly" in the sense that they resemble an insect or minnow or crustacean. No, for mullet I had to tie something that mimicked a Cool Ranch Dorito crumb: some colorful fluff and fuzz that would plop into the water, and hang there in the film for a moment before sinking very slowly, ideally falling right in front of a slurping mullet's mouth as they work in schools right at the surface to hoover up cut grass and other leafy detritus. I have caught two so far. They smell terrible, and their disproportionately huge eyes stare up at me as I remove the small hooks from their fleshy upside-down mouths.

Last time I was fly-fishing for mullet, another person walked up to the bank with a coil of bright-orange rope attached to something softball-size; he swung it out and it splashed into the middle of the bayou, after which he started to slowly retrieve it hand over hand. He was magnet fishing for guns pitched into the bayou after one act of crime or mischief or another.

But I am not walking to fish, today: I have turned away from the bayou and head south on Norman C. Francis, across Canal and Banks and Tulane and over the I-10 highway, streams of traffic flooding east into the city and away westward to the airport and beyond. The foot-and-bike path is in the middle of the bridge, and cars fly by on either side. The sounds and smells are overwhelming at the apex. The view of the downtown is almost majestic.

I pass cyclists, dog walkers, people exercising, dishwashers going to work dressed in all black, junk haulers pushing liberated grocery carts, motorized wheel-chair-assisted people returning from CVS, walkers of all kinds, skaters trailing plumes of skunky weed, walkers, and amblers of all form and kind.

At Claiborne I have to run the gauntlet: fast cars, no crosswalk, a wind-whipped neutral ground minefield separating the lanes. Roads are torn up and marked off, rebar piled up, globs of mis-dumped cement.

I walk past increasingly bigger and nicer houses as I near Tulane, and weave through my neighboring campus before reaching Loyola.

I arrive at my building sweaty, change my shirt, and am ready to teach adventurously.

*   *   *

We've made a life here. I love so many parts of this city, and I have loved raising children here. But I may be reaching my limit. Is it time to move? Fourteen years, and I feel as if I've barely scratched the surface of this place, even as I've tried to pay deep attention and respect to the layers and entanglements of everyday life here. There is still so much to learn. But it is strange to be living in a city that often feels neglected, and self-deprecation is a collective ordinary affect. A city in near ruins, still functioning, while in other parts of the country billionaires spend fortunes on private fantasies of escape and isolation. I'm not looking for an escape. So, stay and dig in? Or try to find a less tenuous respite in which to live, if to only keep up this work of critique and creativity and care?

Reading Chris Dombrowski's moving memoir *The River You Touch*, I run into the dilemma again, as he and his family embark on a big move: "We're ready for an adventure, we had told one another, had assured the kids. But doubt abounded and there were tears from the driveway to the Great Divide" (240). Is a move the adventure, or is the more worthwhile adventure back at home? What are the limits of home as an adventure-place? Where does one even call *home*, in the solastalgic space-time of the Anthropocene?

*   *   *

I see bluegill and cichlids again in the canal.

A month later, oil blooms are again rainbowing the surface of the water. There is no cleanup effort, this time.

Once the fuel washes out, I see the fish though—swimming among waving gnarled vegetation—still here.

Part 3

Final Frontiers

Misadventures in Space

I like reading and teaching novels about adventures, which are by turns cautionary tales and speculative jaunts. And I often find myself planning, initiating, and even occasionally completing more local adventures. But as much as I lightheartedly evoke this word, I've become increasingly suspicious of some of its uses. "Adventure." It's a catchall label, and all too often used to sell crap or propel capitalism on its mad ongoing steamroll. Adventure is a word that can motivate and inspire, but it's also a word that can be used to justify various enterprises—often really unjust and exploitative ones. Increasingly, these enterprises have to do with space travel and all the attendant and often contradictory fantasies therein.

Fred Scharmen's captivating book *Space Settlements* is ostensibly about the idea of technologically elaborate colonies on orbit, resplendently imagined and illustrated in a set of NASA-funded paintings from 1975. This is in some ways the visualization of the mid- to late-twentieth-century adventure of space exploration and inhabitance. But really Scharmen's book is about excavating the granular design history of this particular set of paintings by Don Davis and Rick Guidice, how these images reflected and facilitated a series of conversations, fantasies, and happenings that were less about actual space travel than they were about underlying narratives, unexamined assumptions (often complex political and philosophical), and hidden in plain sight ideas about this pursuit. As one review astutely described Scharmen's more recent book, *Space Forces*, "On a popular science shelf dominated by space mission adventure stories and 'great man' biographies of astronauts and innovators, Scharmen's book stands out"—because it's really about a "history of ideas" more than about technological innovations or actual journeys. Scharmen's books remind me of the Frog and Toad story called "Story," an early primer in metafiction, wherein the "story" of the title ends up being the inability of Toad to think of a story to tell Frog, and the resulting story within a story within a story. As carefully explained by Scharmen, space settlements and space forces are imagined communities, happening already even as they are projected forward and outward. The story of these ideas *is* the adventure, even if the principal actors don't quite realize it.

*   *   *

Julien gets a water rocket for his birthday. The box says, "Be a rocket scientist and launch your first Water Rocket. An easy-to-build science kit specially designed for kids. Let's start your science adventure!" It's not his first one of these; we've built such rockets before out of ordinary two-liter bottles, a rubber stopper, bike pump, and an improvised parachute. They are fun—until they get stuck in the upper branches of maple trees. But this particular version is a slick new set that Camille picked out from a nearby STEM store for kids. Above the picture on the box is a simple tagline: *Play. Read. Inspire.* So much of adventure seems to be about preserving a childlike spirit, while also raising the existential stakes of whatever pursuit is in question.

There was a meme going around for a while that showed how any Lego set—*any* set, even the pink and turquoise suburban-chic Friends line—could be rebuilt as a spaceship. The Lego movie itself lampooned this spaceship craze, with the blue spaceman

Benny who shouts, "Spaceship! Spaceship! Spaceship!" and building these things his only skillset. And I have to admit that when I am playing Legos with my kids, I invariably find myself building . . . spaceships. Or, really, *spacecraft*, as Timothy Morton usefully distinguishes these things:

> A spaceship is large. A spacecraft is small. If it's a boat it's not an Atlantic steamship or an aircraft carrier. A spaceship a consistent crew. In *Star Wars*, the Empire's vessels are quite obviously ships. They are part of an official fleet. There is a large and meticulous class hierarchy on a ship. There's a captain and a crew—if you're on a ship, the captain is at least the master, or lord, lady, duke, duchess . . . of the ship, in charge of punishment and marriage and burial. In space, you see Captains Picard and Kirk officiating at weddings. You hear a whistle that announces that the captain is on deck. A spacecraft is some kind of speedy yacht or catamaran. The work in a spacecraft isn't a job. It's a passion.

In *Toy Story*, Woody sums up this sentiment in a different way when giving Buzz Lightyear a pep-talk about his role in Andy's life: "Woah, hey, wait a minute: being a toy is a lot better than being a space ranger." Of course, Woody hasn't gotten his own movie, yet.

If spacecraft can inspire and get people to play and read—and even to go on science adventures—then I am for them. But when they turn into spaceships—or worse, *star*ships—then we are dealing with something altogether different. Something, in fact, that we're facing now—a space age that would prefer no limits.

We're Already Colonizing Mars

In April 2021 the Ingenuity helicopter took to the Martian air, making it, in NASA's words, "the first attempt at powered, controlled flight of an aircraft on another planet." Or, to put it in more mundane terms, Mars has become another airport. Of course, many crafts have already *landed* on Mars—the most recent carrying the rover Perseverance, with the Ingenuity copter nested inside.

That landing spot was named by the NASA team "Octavia E. Butler Landing." (Official site christenings throughout the solar system must be bestowed by the International Astronomical Union.) At first blush, this seems like a deserved homage to Butler as a visionary artist (for her contributions to the genre of speculative fiction) and as a pathbreaking figure (as the first sci-fi author to receive a MacArthur Fellowship). The name conjoins the daring mission of the Perseverance rover with the legacy of a luminous writer of intellectually daring novels. It also meaningfully honors a Black woman, on behalf of NASA.

However, in the context of Butler's work this appellation becomes deeply complicated. Few writers have been as acutely aware of the moral quandaries of human domination and planetary colonization (see *Dawn*), and how colonies function as palimpsests of slavery and other cross-generational patterns of violence (consider *Kindred*). To call the landing site "Octavia E. Butler Landing" is somewhat ironical; it might as well have been named "Be Careful What You Wish For."

Evoking Butler only highlights the ongoing, fraught conversations around Mars and colonization. Elon Musk has been adamant about the need to get to Mars. The SpaceX webpage titled "Mars & Beyond" quotes Musk's broad ambitions directly: "I can't think of anything more exciting than going out there and being among the stars." This aspirational claim may sound innocent enough, but it assumes we have a right to be there in the first place—indeed, to *colonize* it. Musk argues that in order for humans to survive, it's necessary for the species to become "spacefaring" and "multiplanetary." But colonizing is no innocent practice: Humans have been reckoning with the fraught consequences of colonization on our planet for some time now.

Musk is perhaps the most egregious example of the extraterrestrial colonizing mindset and is an easy target for criticism: another rich white boy who assumes he can conquer the universe, while turning away from systemic problems on Earth. As Andrew Russell and Lee Vinsel bluntly stated in an article at *Aeon:* "At this point in human history, the colonisation of Mars is a distraction from the severe problems facing human societies." And it's notable that Musk does not shy away from calling his plans for Mars "colonization," a word that cannot be disconnected from its brutal legacies.

But even space exploration framed as science instead of colonization risks reproducing troubling patterns. Consider the official view of NASA: "Even if Mars is devoid of past or present life, however, there's still much excitement on the horizon. We ourselves might become the 'life on Mars' should humans choose to travel there one day. Meanwhile, we still have a lot to learn about this amazing planet and its extreme environments." Bowie allusion aside, NASA seems to consider Mars exploration to be both enticing and almost a matter of disinterest ("should humans choose to travel there"). Rover landings on Mars manage to straddle this curious divide, allowing exploration without human presence, while laying the groundwork for future journeys that may indeed involve human settlements. And in the meantime, science-driven exploration is not as neutral as it seems. Marina Koren described the Perseverance mission at the *Atlantic* as "reminiscent of an older way of doing science [where] naturalists and other explorers traveled, welcome or not, to faraway places to gather trunkfuls of specimens for closer study." Even though there are no humans yet on Mars, a pattern of entitlement via science is being established.

If science is the quest to understand nature, then it requires that Mars become *naturalized*. In other words, Mars has to become more Earth-like, in order to rationalize our study (and potential inhabitance of) the planet. In this way, the desert photographs beamed back from Perseverance are hardly simple recordings of what Mars looks like. Rather, they show a non-human nature that we already understand, in a way. As William Cronon explained nearly thirty years ago, such

seemingly natural landscapes are always doing cultural work:
"we too easily imagine that what we behold is Nature when in
fact we see the reflection of our own unexamined longings and
desires." Concomitant with these assumptions are fantasies of
hidden resource reserves, or perhaps even property that can
be declared private, owned, and kept from others. When we
imagine Mars as inhabitable, such fantasies are simmering in
the unconscious of exploration. The desolate horizons and
rocky terrains, cropped and crafted into artfully enhanced
digital images, all but overdetermine the point: Mars is simply
there for the taking, and it's full of possibility. Yet if Mars is a
hypostatized version of earthly Nature, separate from humans,
it is also something we've projected ourselves onto—and to
which we are already laying waste.

Colonialism can be cloaked as a natural impulse to
explore. As science writer Ramin Skibba put it, even in an
article critically interrogating such missions, "Humans love to
explore. It's in our blood." This may sound like common sense,
but it in fact rationalizes elaborate projects that are always
also geopolitical *choices*. With each landing site, discarded
parachute, castoff heat shields, and other debris on the surface;
with all the innumerable images shared on Instagram and
seemingly indifferent recordings of the alien wind tweeted;
with every drone flown (or lost), and each bit of dust gathered
for later examination, humans are continuing the fraught
practice of acting as if we can and should go wherever we
want, take whatever we please, send back postcards . . . and
leave behind our trash.

Edward Abbey, writing in *Desert Solitaire* upon finding
himself "in the middle ground and foreground of the picture"
of Arches National Monument in 1956, declared himself
"sole inhabitant, usufructuary, observer and custodian." From
this vantage point, Abbey wrote in defense of Nature—if
complicatedly so, still aware of his own interloping status.
Abbey's ruminations were always by default colonialist, based
on and protected by governmental power previously exerted
over the land. And at the expense of indigenous populations.

Today we can see traces of Abbey in the Twitter voice and Instagram lens of the rover, nicknamed Percy. (Not to be confused with another Percy, who once warned of the hubris involved when such "lone and level sands stretch far away.") Percy's tweets and pictures share seemingly neutral perspectives, as if the rover just happened to find itself in the Jezero Crater on Mars. These social media feeds are participating in the colonizing of Mars in a more subtle way than leaving behind detritus or inhabiting other peoples' lands. Arguably mere communications and publicity efforts, Percy's online personae nevertheless perpetuate the idea that rolling over it, studying it, snapping pics, collecting . . . it's just what we do, without questioning why we're doing it. "Following" Percy on Mars makes whatever comes next more palatable.

As Mars becomes normalized as a destination for our technology and trash, and as we come to expect social media missives from the Red Planet, its status is shifting in our minds. The planet is not merely revealing itself to humans but being colonized: by our stuff and our accepted ways of seeing and communicating. These may seem like negligible imprints on a relatively barren planet. There's no denying the technical brilliance, innovation, and determination that go into missions like Percy's. But we also should acknowledge the philosophical underpinnings, the implications of which are all too often glossed over. This is how colonizing Mars begins. And even if it seems like no lives are at stake, and no violence is committed there now, we should pause to seriously consider what we take with us, when we continue colonizing places.

*   *   *

When I mentioned what I thought was the odd naming of the landing site to my colleague Scott Heath, who teaches a course on Octavia Butler, he reminded me of the moments in the novel *Parable of the Sower* that reference Mars explicitly. The main character, Lauren Olamina, admires a woman astronaut who made it all the way to Mars only to die tragically there. Butler's Olamina is an emergent prophet, a visionary herself who

believes that "space exploration and colonization are among
the few things left over from the last century that can help
us more than they hurt us." (So it's not just Elon Musk who
champions this vexed notion.)

In Butler's novel, it's 2024 and the world is a postapocalyptic
horrorscape, with environmental disasters rapidly intensifying
and extremist groups committing terrible acts of violence with
impunity. Olamina sees Mars as "heaven in a way . . . but too
nearby, too close within reach of the people who've made such
a hell of life here on Earth." She wants to go way beyond Mars,
beyond anything we've experienced on Earth. She will go on
to found a new religion called Earthseed, which advocates a
radically dynamic idea of existence: for beings not to dwell
on the past or dominate the present but to adapt toward a
future to come. The story makes its indictment of so-called
human progress clear: The twenty-first century of the novel is
a terrifying dystopia hung up on old power structures in many
ways that readers are now calling prophetic.

NASA's space exploration today, while uncannily aligning
with the timeline of *Parable of the Sower*, is decidedly *not* the
vision of the would-be spacefaring Lauren Olamina. Indeed,
as Rebecca Onion once remarked, "You don't have to believe
in space colonization, I don't think, to believe in the idea of
Earthseed."

Parable of the Sower is obviously just a novel—and
Lauren Olamina is not Octavia Butler. But as long as NASA
is channeling the author as honorary, we ought to take her
work seriously. What narratives *are* we committing to as
we carry out the slow march of colonizing Mars? Is Butler's
2024 version of Mars exploration, with a ravaged Earth left
behind, the version that we hope to actually emulate?

*   *   *

When Senator Ted Cruz fled Texas during the polar vortex
that left millions without power and water, it quickly became
a scandal: How could a publicly elected official so brazenly
abandon his people in a time of need? In a bizarre coincidence,

the social media capture of Cruz in the Houston airport occurred on the same day that Percy arrived on Mars. An ill-timed vacation to Mexico and a long-awaited landing on the Red Planet became entangled, as if to expose the truth of both. Cruz is the insensitive colonialist tourist, a self-serving politician out of an Octavia Butler novel; Percy is a scientific wonder as much as another inane internet delight, entertaining people as the world burns.

One early Twitter post from Percy relayed a wind recording on Mars, with Bill Nye's optimistic commentary, "It's out of this world!" Nye's enthusiasm is infectious, and his sentiment genuine. But when science gets conflated with spectacle, and peddled for likes and follows on social media, we need to consider if we're ushering in the next phase of colonization. When colonizing gets repackaged as the latest cool thing, something fun to take part in from afar—especially if you have enough privilege—we should be alert to the histories of violence that come with it. I thought of this again when the code "dare mighty things" was deciphered in the pattern of the now jettisoned parachute. Another social media flurry, one more piece of space garbage, and a further indication that what was happening is nothing less than the colonizing of the Red Planet—on a spot named after a Black writer who well understood the haunting, unresolved problems of colonialism back here on Earth.

If science is the quest to understand nature, one kind of "faraway" nature that is especially susceptible to adventure and exploration, and reverence or protection—but also annihilation—is *wilderness*. Mars is nothing if not a glowing red wilderness prize: thus the "extreme environments" highlighted by NASA. In an *Atlantic* article, Shannon Stirone pointed out that Mars isn't some adventurous hike in the desert, or a long-sought paradise; rather, it's a hellhole. Still, the stretched panorama shots and fuzzy landscapes beamed back from the rover reveal a recycled fantasy of wilderness: Mars as a rugged open place just beckoning to be explored, conquered, and (at least potentially) inhabited.

Imagine if instead of collecting space rocks and leaving defunct rovers and wreckage on Mars, and bombarding internet users with photoshopped pictures, imagine if a different kind of mission took place. Picture one more human journey to the Red Planet, the most ambitious yet, with a rover the size of a shipping container—or better, a garbage truck. We might nickname this rover Frankie, after another literary figure who was tasked with cleaning up a mess made in the name of science. The objective: land on Mars, retrieve every piece of Earth trash—every heatshield, each shredded parachute, all the outmoded rovers—and launch the rover again, detonating it and its amalgam of contents in deep space. We leave tracks, but no junk. And we stop going to Mars, at least for now. For a long now, while we focus instead on Earth. While we really learn how to live on a planet together as a species, alongside myriad other creatures. Earth: this planet that has been our sublime home—and may still be for some time, if we care, if we care for it enough.

Octavia Butler may have been particularly adept at speculating about possible futures of space colonization, and some of her characters might even endorse such journeys, to achieve varying ends. But to harness these visions as destiny or justification would be to make a hubristic mistake right out of one of her fictions, too. Space colonization will bring the thorny problems of Earth colonization along for the ride—we probably just won't see these problems, until it's too late.

The Spacefaring Paradox

If there's one collective lesson gleaned from the Covid pandemic so far, it may be the shared difficulty of being isolated in one's own home—whether alone or with family members or roommates. The stresses of quarantine included crushing mundane routines, personal habits hypostatized, and all-too-familiar views (stove range, bathroom mirror, that solitary tree outside, changing while nothing changed). As Amanda

Mull wrote in the Atlantic, after working from home for a year, her "wallpaper has begun to yellow." When space closes in, humans tend not to thrive. It can drive us to the brink of craziness.

I've been thinking about this problem in relation to SpaceX and its rapid advancements throughout the pandemic, including the most recent successful launch and landing of its largest rocket, Starship. This was a prototype of the ship that Musk intends to travel to the Moon, to Mars, and eventually beyond. In "crew mode" it will be able to carry up to 100 passengers. As Marina Koren reported for the Atlantic, Elon Musk suddenly seems a lot closer to his goal of making humans "a multiplanetary species." If there was something vaguely cathartic or even inspiring in Musk's tenacious drive to perfect the SpaceX Starship, *especially during the pandemic*, it may have been the fantasy of more space, out there, beyond the constraints of Earth which were felt so heavily in 2020.

Yet there's a paradox lurking at the core of SpaceX.

Before SpaceX will take passengers to space, the company plans to offer "Earth to Earth transportation." These would be ridiculously quick rides around the world—for instance, London to New York in a half-hour. The idea is to launch the rocket with paying travelers above Earth's atmosphere, then speed around the globe and land promptly at the destination. As the SpaceX website boasts, "Imagine most journeys taking less than 30 minutes with access to anywhere in the world in an hour or less." (Of course, this "anywhere in the world" really means major urban centers with an appropriate landing pad and equipment to service the rocket, but we'll let the hyperbole slide.)

If achieved at commercial scale, this would turn the airline industry upside down—or at the very least, it would be a massive disruption for airlines that rely heavily on long-haul flights. No other airline or aircraft manufacturer is currently developing a similar mode of transit. A company called Boom recently made headlines for its attempt to bring back supersonic commercial flight, with a plane that is reminiscent of the Concorde, but for fliers on a budget. Yet SpaceX's Starship flights, if realized, would make supersonic feel like the slow train.

The rationale for speeding up long flights, naturally, is that it is widely understood that people do not like to be in cramped airplane cabins for more than an hour. The less time, the better. The history of commercial aviation has been a race to shorten the time from origin to destination and make more efficient all the steps in between. Still, there are some things that can't be fixed. No one likes a tarmac delay or a long flight involving an annoying seatmate or constant turbulence. Time stretches out and plays tricks on the mind when you're sitting in an airplane.

Here is where the paradox enters. The same Starship that promises faster air travel around our planet—eliminating those pesky five-, ten-, or fifteen-hour flights—is also the aspirational repository for Musk's would-be passengers to Mars. In other words, the Starship cabin is not ultimately intended for trips "under an hour" but in fact for journeys of multiple months. If you think air rage is bad on a short hop from Las Vegas to San Diego, just wait until your seatmates are there beside you for weeks on end, in the black void of space. SpaceX describes the interior of these craft as including "private cabins, large common areas, centralized storage, solar storm shelters and a viewing gallery." This makes it sound not so bad. Still, there's no getting around the blunt truth of containment over a long period of time. Those "large" common areas are likely to shrink the longer the trip takes.

Then there's sleep. Between 2007 and 2011 the European Space Agency worked with Russia to simulate the conditions of a trip to Mars, particularly as a psychological isolation experiment. Called Mars500, the longest part of this study ran between 2010 and 2011; it revealed a significant degradation of the simulacral explorers' sleep patterns. While on widebody airliners a business class cocoon seat can deliver comfort (and even luxury) during an overnight flight, such ergonomic palliatives won't be as easy for a yearlong journey. Space travel to Mars is supposed to be a bold and daring adventure. But what if it ends up feeling more like a super long redeye flight?

For years Musk has compared his rockets to airliners, using the familiar sizes and thrust capacities of Boeing 737s and 747s as reference points for his future-bound ships. These comparisons circulate on social media, by way of making SpaceX craft both more graspable *and* more impressive. But the analogies are telling. As much as the goal is to reduce the time of feeling trapped inside a cramped cabin, the end game is in fact *more* of this time. And let's be honest: a hab on Mars is not going to be a whole lot more spacious than the interior of the ship.

If the dream of space travel involves new horizons and feelings of unbound freedom—to explore, to discover, to spread humanity—there is a nightmare lurking just around the corner of consciousness. There will be no real "arrival" on this fantasy trip: it is enclosures and pressurized chambers all the way down. When it comes to human space travel, the destination really is the journey. And the journey will be long, and claustrophobic. As far as "quarantine" goes, spacefaring may feel familiar to those who lived through the Covid pandemic—and certain survival tactics may crossover.

Musk wants to send humans to Mars (and beyond) because he believes that the species is doomed on Earth, sooner or later. This bleak assessment belies two haunting presuppositions: the miserable masses will wither on a climate scorched and ecologically damaged planet back home; meanwhile, the spacefaring select will find themselves in a whole new purgatory of cramped isolation, en route and wherever they "land."

The wish image of habitations on other planets is for simulated environments that feel as good as—if not better than—our home planet. The reality is bound to be precarious and highly contingent—no matter how awesome and intact space settlements might appear in artistic renderings. The motivation for spacefaring is, at least for Musk, premised on a desire to escape a planet in limbo, but the alternative is hardly a safe haven. This is the paradox of spacefaring: it's a lose-lose proposition.

As anthropologist Lisa Messeri has found in her research on planetary scientists, ideas about inhabiting outer space can tend to revert back to making sense of our place on Earth. This isn't necessarily a bad thing; in fact, one of the arguments for space exploration is to improve life back home. Yet as SpaceX moves closer to sending humans beyond the space station, beyond the moon, it's worth pausing to consider the real implications of these endeavors. We're already "spacefaring," in a literal sense of the term. We know what it feels like to cram ourselves in tight vessels or rooms, and we don't generally like it. And as the pandemic gradually (hopefully) subsides, our interconnectedness as a species and entanglements with other life forms have been made vivid. The adventures and challenges of spacefaring are right before our eyes, the spinning ground on which we're already standing.

Rocket Men

"I've heard about space for a long time now," the actor William Shatner announced on the blog of Blue Origin, the space exploration company founded by Amazon's Jeff Bezos. "I'm taking the opportunity to see it for myself. What a miracle."

These remarks are conspicuously lacking in the high-flown touch of the late Gene Roddenberry, creator of Captain James T. Kirk, the beloved character played by Shatner on *Star Trek*. Roddenberry was given to making dreamy pronouncements like "The human adventure is just beginning." In any case Life was scheduled to imitate Art when the ninety-year-old Shatner would blast off on Blue Origin's New Shepard suborbital launch vehicle. The cinematic spaceman, by spending ten minutes in (or at least near) space, would thus represent the embodiment of an "exploration of futurism"—a monumental performance of nostalgia for the early, romantic days of space travel, and for the glamor and sense of discovery conjured by the memory of *Star Trek*.

In this way Shatner's space flight isn't so much a PR gimmick as it is a fashion statement; he's like a Starfleet badge for Jeff Bezos to wear. The billionaire's lifelong devotion to *Star Trek* is well known; he appeared as an alien in the 2016 film *Star Trek Beyond*, and a few years ago Redditors traced the original 8-foot studio model of the Starship Enterprise to Blue Origin's headquarters in Kent, Washington.

The BBC reported that years ago, Shatner turned down an offer from Richard Branson, another billionaire space mogul, to fly into space on Virgin Galactic, because he'd been asked to pay for the privilege. "He wanted me to go up and pay for it and I said: 'Hey, you pay me and I'll go up. I'll risk my life for a large sum of money.'" John Herrman reported that Blue Origin told *The New York Times* that "Mr. Shatner would be flying 'as our guest'—meaning he didn't pay for his ticket." (How much is it worth to Blue Origin, already the vanity project of a galactically self-absorbed man, the richest on earth, to appease his vanity with the childhood dream of being space pals with Captain Kirk?) Bezos's own performance as a spaceman some weeks prior was roundly mocked as absurdly affected. The cowboy hat alone made it plain how much the *pose* mattered to Bezos.

Marina Koren's shrewd take at *The Atlantic* on Elon Musk's most recent SpaceX launch likewise spoke of the *style* of billionaire space tourism. Describing the recent Inspiration4 commercial mission, she noted that space travel has become "a real customer experience. You can see it in the Dragon's interior—the minimalist design, all clean lines, with touch-screen displays and cushy fabrics." It's not just about the blast-off; it's about textures, design, lines—being in space comes with a certain futuristic look, recalling movies like *Ex Machina*, or a hotel designed by Philippe Starck.

*   *   *

Science and technology drive space travel, but getting people to care about it requires expertise and elegance in manipulating aesthetic registers: futuristic fantasies and desires must be

visualized and projected into our collective imagination to
stoke excitement and feelings of awe, every bit as much as
they need to be realized, tested, and fine-tuned by engineers.
Shatner's voyage with Blue Origin kept this admixture swirling.
As *The New York Times* reported, audiences would witness a
"blurring of reality and fiction."

This helps explain why Kara Swisher, in a recent interview
for Sway, kept trying to pin down David Eggers on what it
would take for him to join an actual space launch, suggesting
that it would be a significant matter for a novelist to visit space.
"What would you do if Jeff Bezos offered you a seat on his
rocket ship, for example?" she asked, a question tangentially
related to his latest dystopian novel *The Every*. "I'm always a
fan of space exploration and I'm the biggest NASA geek," he
replied.

> And so anything that moves the ball forward a little bit
> there—I think that the absurdity of Bezos spending what
> could have been people's wages on a rocket is—no one
> could have satirized that, especially the phallic rocket. It's
> so far beyond Mike Myers . . .

> But overall, when Richard Branson does his rocket, I want
> to see it. I want to see what Elon Musk is doing with his
> rocket program. I think that there is a way to do it that is
> valuable to humanity.

Even through his equivocations—"*anything* that moves the
ball forward . . . there is *a way* to do it"—Eggers acknowledges
that space travel is not just about flashy tech but about image
and messaging as well as political realities, and the idea that
exploration itself might potentially be "valuable to humanity."

Stories and art about space travel significantly predated
the real thing, but it's been about spectacle since the days of
Jules Verne; it's rhetorical—and entertaining. Russia is about
to make the first-ever fictional movie filmed in space. Not to
be outdone, last year NASA announced a collaboration with

Tom Cruise to film a movie in space: "We need popular media to inspire a new generation of engineers and scientists." Young technologists are as inspired by the rhetoric of fashion, art, and storytelling as anyone else is. The danger is that the aesthetic seductions of minimalist design and special, fancy costumes with your name embroidered on the chest will overwhelm what is essentially a pernicious message.

Virgin Galactic's Richard Branson boasted after his company's first fully crewed launch that "the new commercial space industry is poised to open the universe to humankind," upon which the critic Ian Bogost replied dryly, "This is the opposite of what has happened today." It's painfully obvious that Branson's rocket ship is for the very, very few. But it can—indeed it must—look cool to all, as long the elite are the ones who will benefit.

* * *

In my neighborhood art museum gift shop recently, I spotted a toy called Build Your Own Mars Colony. ("Simply unfold the poster to reveal the surface of Mars, pop out the pieces and assemble them, no scissors or glue required, for hours of extraterrestrial fun.") The toy is creative and playful, though it celebrates the instrumental and scientific. It incorporates aesthetic elements of "design." Midway through Kim Stanley Robinson's monumental novel *Red Mars*, a minor character dismisses the job of colonizing Mars as "artwork." This idea echoed in my head as I pondered the little cardboard kit.

Around the same time, I saw a headline about NASA paying people to spend a year living in a simulated Martian habitat. The article at *Business Insider* led with an "artist's rendering" of a simulacral Red Planet. In mid-2021, well into the second year of the Covid pandemic, the futility of this fantasy was almost palpable. As if living on Earth wasn't hard enough! Somehow the government had decided that it was worth paying someone a salary *to pretend to live on Mars*. The more immediately beneficial fantasy would be to pay people to live on Earth. But that would not be a spectacle, something to *watch*, to contemplate aesthetically as well as technically. (On the other hand, simulated Mars habs are a topos already rife with earthbound drama.)

Lego currently offers not one but two sets featuring the Space Shuttle, an outmoded vehicle that nevertheless continues to captivate the imagination—not as functioning technology but as a symbol. Legos are toys, but they are also cultural artifacts, even a kind of art; the company increasingly recognizes this as their fans age into adults. After last summer's first successful SpaceX launch of the Dragon with astronauts inside, the capsule was christened the Endeavor, in homage to the retired Space Shuttle—keeping the ambience of the program alive in name, if not in form. The Space Shuttle is the image of a dream we're desperate to keep alive, of American ingenuity, frontiersmanship, daring, and future-mindedness. Adventure.

This brings us back to SpaceX's recent launch: the Inspiration4 mission. Elon Musk's company no longer needs to publicize the spectacle of a successful launch: this is old hat. The latest mission had a new appeal, though: it was the first time four civilians went up in space, opening the market up to commercial launches. When the space tourists returned safely to Earth, a new type of commodity came into being, a new, almost inconceivably rare new look to wear. (No matter if the SpaceX outfits are themselves derivative, somewhere between Biker Scout chic and bleached Daft Punk.) Yet space fashion is already utterly effete, worn out, as the choice of the ninety-year-old Shatner for Blue Origin's launch—paying homage to the 57-year-old Jeff Bezos's personal nostalgia for *Star Trek*—so clearly demonstrates. Not only have the billionaires stolen our space sex, as the philosopher Margret Grebowicz has argued, they're also recycling space style, in a kind of billionaires' Buffalo Exchange.

*   *   *

On my eighth birthday, the space shuttle *Challenger* exploded. We were sitting in our classroom watching the launch on TV, eating Cheerios out of little paper cups. A teacher, Christa

McAuliffe, was on board; it was supposed to be a historic moment. But not in this way. The visual, aesthetic registers of space flight, the explosion and spiraling wisps of white smoke, were burned into my inner mind in that moment. How it looks versus how it's supposed to look. It was and is a story of human ingenuity and courage, discovery, and the leading edges of science and technology. But the *Challenger* disaster unexpectedly became the story of how we visualize each precarious, potentially treacherous journey beyond our atmosphere. It's a story of what our space voyagers look like— and when such looks take on new meanings.

Fashion and design can revolutionize the way we inhabit space, or move in our bodies. But these things can also be banal, numbing, and fascistic. The aesthetic intrigue of space travel is fading now—throttled, like so much else, by the choking effects of excessive wealth and human narcissism. It is starting to seem more and more like a ratty and recognizable affect. Space travel: that entertaining *look* that billionaires give off. Rare, and hopelessly uncool.

Space Tourism and Nature Writing

When William Shatner returned on October 13, 2021, from his four minutes in suborbital space he was effusive, to say the least: "What you've given me is the most profound experience." He was struck by "how vulnerable Earth looked from that altitude." Tearful with joy, Shatner phrased his feelings somewhat contortedly: "I'm so filled with emotion with what just happened. . . . I hope I never recover from this." To *recover* makes it sound like an injury occurred. What exactly happened to Captain Kirk up there?

Shatner's postlaunch comments reflected a powerful, if vague, sort of ecological awareness: "Everyone needs to have the philosophical understanding of what we're doing to Earth." I was struck by this claim in particular, as it resonated with a book I happened to be teaching the week of the Blue Origin launch.

In a seminar called Ecological Thought, my students and I were reading and discussing Douglas Chadwick's *Four Fifths a Grizzly*, a book that promises (according to its subtitle) to offer "a new perspective on nature that just might save us all." The book blends travel writing, basic ecology, and biology lessons with fabulous photo spreads and textbook-like informational callouts. It is a *beautiful* book, materially speaking—and it seems to assume that such beauty, carefully rendered and reproduced, can be harnessed to jolt the reader into a state of environmental enlightenment. It might just work. It's a residue of that Romantic fantasy of Nature as the ideal teacher—and yet, it's a fantasy that even the Romantics were keenly self-critical about. See *Frankenstein*. See Wordsworth. See Blake, whose poem "Auguries of Innocence" begins with images of natural enlightenment and sublimity but devolves into a kind of mortal delirium.

The publisher of *Four Fifths a Grizzly*, the high-end outdoor apparel company Patagonia, itself feeds off Romantic tropes of extreme wilderness, solitary reflection, and sublime views. But the company is also clear about its attempts to be more modern, espousing environmental activism in place of (or at least in tandem with) rash consumerism. Patagonia, even while implicated in advanced consumer culture, is blunt about the fact that ecosystems are at risk around the planet. This is where *Four Fifths a Grizzly* ostensibly intervenes.

The thesis of Chadwick's book is that nature is not something "out there" but is intimately a part of us—part of everything. This perspective, while not exactly *new*, is in line with texts from disparate disciplines that we had studied in our class. So far, so good. *Four Fifths a Grizzly* is also a colossal mess. It tries to do too much, feels incredibly underedited, doesn't deliver on its cover promises, and is ridiculously overdesigned.

One of my students noted that it was trying too hard to be a coffee table book, another student called the book a "massive fail," and a third suggested that it was a book for suburbanites who fly to Colorado once a year to go skiing. Another student pointed out how apolitical it was: while it professes to be intellectually interested in threats to biodiversity, there's barely a mention of climate change or pollution—much less our own responsibility for these things. Yet one more student pointed out that one of the photographs (on page 102) *is an actual ad for Patagonia.* My students are smart, and they know smarm when they see it.

I was trying to temper my students' reactions so that they'd see how the book's themes were basically in line with those of the other books we were reading; the style and intended audience were just different, I opined. There are moments of good travel writing in the book and delightful instances of scientific wonder (such as Chadwick's extended essay on strawberries). But, on the whole, I had to agree with my students: there was something unsettlingly retro about the book, even as it is pitched as a forward-looking compilation.

On the last text-page of the book, an extended photo caption explains what readers will find on the following pages: "The aquanaut and the astronaut: the planktonic larva of a brittle star and Bruce McCandless II, making the first untethered space walk, February 3, 1984. Different as they might seem in some respects, both of these life forms are free-floating and both are made from the very same stuff: water and stardust" (269). What follows are two photographs: on the verso page a close-up of the larva of an echinoderm (related to a starfish), and on the recto page, a photograph of the astronaut floating in space.

The images echo one another: two beings with legs and arms, drifting. The implicit suggestion is that grasping nature is always a matter of scale and attention: depending on how zoomed in or out you are, you see (and appreciate) different things—and you realize that everything is interconnected. (Again, not a novel idea: Charles and Ray Eames showed this in their 1977 film, *Powers of Ten.*)

We were finishing *Four Fifths a Grizzly* on the day that Shatner took off in the New Shephard spacecraft, AKA "the dick rocket," making the aquanaut and the astronaut more than an illuminating juxtaposition. It was also weirdly consonant with Shatner's takeaway of the Blue Origin launch. Does the rarefied view from above Earth amount to the same thing as looking closely at a small organism? Can both these spectacles result in a profound ecological epiphany? Is space travel a new kind of nature writing?

To pair with *Four Fifths a Grizzly*, I gave my students a few excerpts from Ross Gay's *The Book of Delights*, a lyrical collection of "essayettes" that record daily "delights" the author encounters over a year of his life (2015–16). Gay's short narratives often involve fruits, flowers, and other vegetal life—which I thought might help us make real some of the more abstruse connections that Chadwick is trying to communicate.

But Gay teaches us something different. To pay attention to the world—even when *delighting* in it—is also to see and take note of social problems and pernicious systems. It is to recognize deep structural inequalities and patterns of violence. It is to realize that even among all this beauty, we're still in a mess that's anything but apolitical.

Humans used to do or think a lot of things that most of us now consider wrong: slavery, public executions, brutally colonizing lands, wiping out entire animal populations, believing the Earth is flat, imagining stars as holes in the sky, and so on. These practices and beliefs are anathema to what it means to be a modern human in the twenty-first century. Today space travel has passionate proponents, and some of them think it's our destiny—the only way for humans to survive their otherwise inevitable extinction on this planet.

Chadwick's book holds out hope for a more sustainable form of coexistence on Earth, even as it shies away from thornier environmental problems in the present. The title, *Four Fifths a Grizzly*, serves as a koan for a larger lesson: *all* beings share life with *every* other entity. Space travel off Earth may seem earnest in its attempt to continue life and spread this organic world. But such launches might also turn out to be something we look back at with bemusement. *What were people thinking?*

Didn't we realize with every rocket that blasted billionaires into orbit, we were ignoring the very ground that sustains us? Even arguably accelerating environmental catastrophe?

After his brief visit to space, William Shatner was widely quoted saying, "Everybody in the world needs to do this." It almost sounds like the subtitle of Douglas Chadwick's book. But it could also be turned on its head, in the spirit of Ross Gay's essayettes: if it's about taking sheer delight and finding humility in the face of the planet, everybody is *already* able to do this. Look around. Pay attention. Take care. But you don't need to go to space to "do this." And however sublime, views of nature don't absolve humans of the problems we've caused.

Part 4

The Ends of Adventure

I am not sure when exactly I became interested in the concept of adventure, but I think it probably happened around the same time that I started paying close attention to airports. Or at least, that's when I started tuning into this idea more. Something about the rent between place and home, and no-place and away—in fact, finishing this book I realize now that I am writing a follow-up to my 2019 book *Searching for the Anthropocene*, which I might have also called *Human Adventure (vol. 1)*. But let me try to map some earlier points of this inquiry, as well.

When I moved to Bozeman, Montana, in 2001, I was looking for a job to pay the rent before I started graduate school. I had been patching together seasonal rafting and kayak guiding jobs, but I needed something more stable. So when I saw an ad in the paper for a job with United Airlines, I drove over to the airport and picked up a paper application form. I applied, interviewed, and got the position. My title was *cross-utilized agent*. Twenty-plus years later, I still love the sound of that job description: *cross-utilized agent*. The title alone sounded adventurous.

It was a fascinating job, if also just hard work with punishingly early and late shifts. But it gave me deep insight into the everyday operations and behind-the-scenes drama of airport life. These were never simply runways, baggage carts, and fifty-seater regional jets; no, to me in such scenes I saw a swirling matrix of environmental attitudes, geographical desires, cultural aesthetics, and logistical networks. These were the frontiers of the early twenty-first century—and not just the airports out in the American West but how they connected to every other runway pattern imprinted on the planet.

I started working there in the spring of 2001. Airports were different, then. You could show up, buy a ticket, and be on a plane soaring over the country an hour later. Security changed dramatically after 9/11, but past the checkpoints, airports remained sites of adventure in themselves: they were little worlds offering secret enclaves and surprise encounters. But airports have accreted into something else, of late.

Ann Patchett has a question in her latest book *These Precious Days* that I've been mulling over ever since I read it: "Remember when it was still possible to get lost in an airport?" This recollection has to do with something indirectly related to air travel: it's about the proliferation of smartphones, about having maps and directions always at one's fingertips. With the rise of personal communications devices and online information networks, what were previously challenging landscapes have become thoroughly mapped and made more easily navigable. Or at least that's the expectation. Airports can still be maddening, a fact that I'm perhaps weirdly thankful for.

I ended up studying airports and air travel in American literature and culture, and eventually writing four books directly on this topic. And the idea of adventure was always lurking right under the surface of the runways, check-in counters, and gate areas. Airports: what better place to observe people embarking on, or returning from, adventures?

To be clear, my take on airports over the years has been persistently, if increasingly, critical. I think that human flight has become built up and ingrained to the point that it is almost impossible to imagine other forms of transportation at scale and that the normalization of commercial air travel has resulted (and I realize this sounds counterintuitive) in more human *dis*connection. Additionally, the environmental impacts of human flight are significant. Of course, there are moments of genuine humanity and kindness that happen on airplanes (and less often, in airports), but overwhelmingly the experience of commercial flight, for most travelers, is barely tolerated irritation and multiple forms of physical and psychological discomfort. And yet it remains a cultural practice curiously upheld as a pinnacle of progress.

I don't deny the technical miracle of flight and all the engineering feats that make human aviation possible. I appreciate aerial views, as well as the necessary skillsets of pilots. I still fly, though I am attempting to limit my own trips more and more. Two trips a year at most seems like a sensible limit. The adventure of human flight perhaps does not need to end entirely, but it could use some new, intentional limits. As Ian Bogost writes in his book *Play Anything*, "Limits aren't limitations, not absolute ones. They're just the stuff out of which stuff is made" (203). It sounds obvious to state it this way, but we have made air travel what it is today; with new limits in mind, we could reimagine and refashion flight.

One of the more compelling arguments in support of air travel that I sometimes hear has to do with environmental awareness. It goes like this: When humans fly to visit new parts of the world, they can develop appreciation for unfamiliar geographies, exotic ecosystems, and different cultures. And this appreciation can then rebound back to one's own place, enhancing environmental ethics and responsibility at home. It is a persuasive line of reasoning: if only everyone could take a perfect trip to a new place and learn these lessons from it. If only everyone could have such an adventure.

The problem, though, is all the so-called "flyover" space in-between. Land or water below, seen from 30,000 feet, becomes so much space to tune out. And similarly, the sociality of the in-between zones that are the airport and the airplane—this too becomes disposable. So, it can be hard to build an environmental ethic from a basis of high-speed flyover consumption. As Ann Patchett hints at, we've also almost entirely forgotten how to treat the journey itself as an adventure—even the most boring parts of it: the waiting and wandering aimlessly in a cavernous airport. To quote Ian Bogost again, "The 'fun' of a flight, it would seem, comes from the ordinary and the extraordinary all at once" (65). But all too often, one gets beaten down by the drudgery or amped up by the drama—it's difficult to balance the ordinary and the extraordinary while in transit.

Bogost also makes this provocative claim about air travel: "While no one would wish to be on a flight in which a real danger to cabin, crew, and passengers were to take place, the idea of encountering one is not much different that the deliberate pursuit of other risky adventures, such as skydiving or theme-park thrill rides" (71). In other words, even though we may have become mostly numb to the danger and risk that come with air travel, a *sense* of adventure is always on a low simmer in these most mundane experiences.

*   *   *

Where do we find adventure, these days? And how are desires for adventure linked to environmental awareness? Some current advertising campaigns offer insight into these questions. Insight, but also further dilemmas.

A recent Free People catalog displayed a new line of their Movement apparel called the Adventure Collection. Against mountainous backgrounds, fashion models tromp with backpacks, fleece jumpers, hats, water bottles, and boots. The tagline for this series of items is "Adventure Awaits." The small print on the opening page reads, "Join us this season as we explore the country's most iconic parks—follow @fpmovement. SHOP OUR ADVENTURE COLLECTION." A QR code floats beneath these words, superimposed over the far bank of a wide river. The invitation is to spectate, to follow, to purchase—to tap repeatedly on a phone screen. The image is something of a trick photo: the rippling water, the green hill on the far shoreline, the chill in the air suggested by the jacket and cap—these aren't where the adventure lies. Or, the adventure is at least split in two directions: outside and online.

Such a curious phrase: *adventure awaits*. Does this mean that once we purchase the items we see on these pages, we will be able to *go* on an adventure, too? Or could it possibly mean that the model on the page is *about* to go on an adventure—but it hasn't happened quite yet? Is this catalog a portal to adventure, to seeing what adventure can look like? Or is it, in all its Romantic imagery, a mere red herring that deploys "adventure" as a consumerist fantasy object that always recedes past a reachable horizon? And what is the *time* of adventure? Must there always be a part of adventure that *awaits*, in other words, an elusive finality to this objective?

It's funny how the images in this catalog show the models basically loafing, standing around, kicking in water, and not quite *using* the outdoor equipment on display. Those flies stuck on the bucket hat, that empty net, jackets draped instead of tightly zipped against the elements. A fly rod dangled over the water, grip still in its factory seal. In other words, the adventure here really does seem to await a time to come. Still, there is an effort on the company's behalf to make consumers more aware of the "iconic parks"—presumably, a low-key conservationist message is baked into the product line. But adventure, such as it is, remains off the page, inaccessible. The rugged landscape is rendered a fashion runway, an aesthetic screen more than some real place where actual adventures might occur.

*   *   *

We may want to seek a real runway in order to find adventure.

At the Delta website I see it in bold, encouraging web surfers to fly again as the Covid pandemic slowly subsides, interpellating would-be travelers: "Ready for adventure?" A picture above these words shows an alpine lake edged with lodgepole pines, and a valley swooping up to a mountain ridge with snowy chutes, in the distance. It is an idealized location for adventure—a place that would immediately result in clarity of the mind and which calls for peak bodily performance.

And then, again—the fine print: "The world is open for travel so start planning your next adventure. Explore our best flight deals and get out into the world." In this ad spot is so much of what irritates me about the enterprise of air travel: as if one is not already always "in" the world! The wording suggests that the world is *open*, like a shop having been closed for some reason (don't mention the plague). This misconception abounded during the pandemic, the notion of *closure* becoming synonymous with various temporary measures put in place (however falteringly and inconsistently) for the sake of public health.

Clicking on this ad, I am directed to a slightly different elaboration of the same sales pitch: "Plan your next adventure today. Every adventure starts with a plan. Take advantage of these flight deals and start your next vacation—sooner than you think." These words are adorned with a different picture: a European village, with rows of buildings and an old stone bridge crossing an emerald river. The sun is low on the horizon. And this *sooner than you think*: another kind of temporal uncertainty.

In these two images, we see how the Great Outdoors is often set in a chiasmic dynamic with Culture, and indeed cultural *difference*. The implication is that encountering adventure can happen with no other humans around, *or* in the midst of humans who are different from you. Air travel becomes the passage through which such experience can be had: plan your next adventure today.

The poet Claudia Rankine has also identified air travel as a means for cultural broadening and exchange. Only for Rankine, the site of interest is the space-time of transit itself. In an essay from her perspective as a Black woman investigating white male privilege, Rankine writes:

> it occurred to me that I tend to be surrounded by white men I don't know when I'm traveling, caught in places that are essentially nowhere: in between, en route, up in the air. As I crisscrossed the United States, Europe and Africa giving talks about my work, I found myself considering these white men who passed hours with me in airport lounges, at gates, on planes. They seemed to me to make up the largest percentage of business travelers in the liminal spaces where

we waited. That I was among them in airport lounges and in first-class cabins spoke in part to my own relative economic privilege, but the price of my ticket, of course, does not translate into social capital.

Places that are essentially nowhere. It's quite an indictment of these sites that are secured and protected unlike almost any other quasi-public space. Rankine harnesses these "liminal" zones to confront awkward situations and ask hard questions about structural racism.

This is no abstraction for Rankine, but a real condition of being a Black woman in a place that would seem to have a naturalized order of people. In turn, Rankine's essay unfolds like the best nature writing: reporting the encounters and episodes that stand metonymically for a vaster ecosystem. If wild nature and built culture exist on a chiasmic continuum, as the Delta website suggests, then Rankine troubles the exact point of crossover: what is natural and thus subject to evolutionary long-time, and what is socially constructed and therefore able to be addressed, redressed, and changed?

After a tense but sustained exchange about racism and privilege with a white male seatmate, a discussion that ranges widely across their respective personal narratives, and which reaches a point—however tentative—of mutual respect, Rankine closes her essay with the following thoughts: "I was pleased he could carry the disturbance of my reality. And just like that, we broke open our conversation—random, ordinary, exhausting and full of a shared longing to exist in less segregated spaces."

This "shared longing" emerges through, if not exactly from, the close confines of air travel. Rankine focuses on the "liminal spaces" of airports and airplanes—a focused and intense space-time, in turn. If adventure, including cultural broadening, is that which awaits, Rankine calls the bluff: No, let's try to confront things *now*, even as we're "up in the air."

In *Jim Crow Terminals: The Desegregation of American Airports*, historian Anke Ortlepp traces the rise and fall of segregated airports in the US south, from the late 1940s to the early 1960s. Ortlepp "conceives of airport terminals as sites of conflict—as territories of confrontation over the renegotiation of racial identities in postwar America" (10). For civil rights activists, but also for African American travelers trying merely to exercise their citizenship and status as travelers, "the airport terminal was new protest territory." (37) Tracing a series of legal cases and drawing on oral histories and government documents, Ortlepp paints a vivid picture of how civil rights debates played out inconsistently (and often indirectly) around the planning, construction, and operation of new terminals throughout the southern United States in the postwar period.

One of the most curious minor details in *Jim Crow Terminals* is the reoccurring function of the *delay*. Numerous cases cited in Ortlepp's book, wherein a traveler is either denied service or offered a separate dining area, are triggered by the occasion of a delayed flight: "When the return flight of her business trip from New York to Washington was delayed . . ." (16); "Faced with a delay . . ." (39); "While waiting for a delayed flight . . ." (67); "While waiting for his delayed connecting flight . . ." (69). Each of these unplanned, extra temporalities at an airport results in an altercation or a confrontation in which segregation is imposed—and then held to legal account. In other words, one of the banes of air travel—the dreaded delay—in a bizarre way ends up *aiding* the desegregation of Jim Crow terminals. Hiding in plain sight here is a quite radical reconceptualization of one of modernity's most annoying low-grade glitches: time to kill becomes time for social justice.

Claudia Rankine's recent work operates similarly in the delayed spatiotemporal realm of waiting to fly, then waiting *while* flying. Contra an airline's sales pitch to travel to a destination in order to experience otherness, to broaden one's mind—be that a remote mountain range or a distant village— the real "sites of conflict," in Ortlepp's words, are staring us in the face already: contact with nature, as well as inclusion and justice, must be found in airports and airplanes, if they are to be found anywhere at all. Adventure is not that which awaits but which is happening with/in the very social environment we already inhabit. Awareness of this always-closer landscape is the true challenge. And it doesn't require a ticket to fly anywhere. Or at least a ticket always involves multiple registers of adventure.

*   *   *

The latest Orvis catalog flops through my mail slot. I reluctantly turn the pages, by turns enamored with the fancy gear and put off by garish displays of wealth and privilege. I pause, though, when I get to an odd 3/4-page photograph of a grungy, white fly-fisherman standing on an airport tarmac, facing the nose of a widebody Airbus nuzzled up to a jet bridge. What's an airport doing here? The caption reads, "Ian Provo, staring down that giant aircraft and knowing that the bush plane just off camera is where the real adventure begins. The Amazon Jungle." The image is one of semiotic overload: the plane, the vehicles, the would-be adventurer . . . . And yet apparently the *real* adventure is not even pictured here. Adventure awaits, again.

One interesting thing to me about this image is how it lingers on the workzone of the airport. It gestures toward logistics, labor, and technical matters that are so often glossed over when we talk about adventure. We even see an airport worker standing on the scissors lift—a nod, perhaps, to the fact that not *everyone* can be on vacation. This scene, as disjunctive as it may seem within the pages of a high-end gear catalog, works almost like the unconscious of adventure. The words state that the real adventure begins "just off camera"—but what the camera has *captured* suggests that the adventure is already right in front of us, too.

A dozen pages earlier in the catalog, there is an advertisement for a collaboration between Orvis and an organization called Brown Folks Fishing. It is called "Angling for All." A blurb reads:

> In summer 2020, Brown Folks Fishing (BFF), an organization committed to building community and expanding access

among Black, Indigenous, and People of Color (BIPOC) in
fishing and its industry, launched the Angling for All Pledge
with Orvis as the inaugural pledge. The pledge seeks to
dismantle systemic barriers to entry and participation at all
levels of the fishing industry. Learn more at orvis.com

Behind a Black fly-fisherman in the photograph, the buildings
of downtown Minneapolis rise up. Again, the country/city,
nature/culture chiasmus is revealed. If fishing, and fly-fishing
in particular, is often isolated in a rarefied far-off realm, then
the capacious phrasing of "and its industry" scatters out to
everywhere else. And if outdoor sports are typically white-
presenting, Orvis is overtly attempting to change the image,
here.

Yet eerily like the Free People opener for their Adventure
Collection, the next step from the catalog page is to . . . go
online. Not *get outside and enjoy nature now!* Not *learn about
white privilege.* No: just go online. Of course, there's a definite
difference between these two ad campaigns, and Orvis appears
to be taking a contemporary issue very seriously: dismantling
systemic barriers with respect to people of color. But this
project of social justice complicates any easy sense of what the
primary activity is, here.

Fly-fishing is the obvious marketing hook throughout this
catalog: another two-page spread advertises Orvis Adventures,
guided trips to perfect locations. "Great adventures start here."
But the need for societal change lingers over these pages and
interrupts gear sales quite overtly. Not unlike the eccentric
airport tarmac later in the catalog, Orvis gives significant page-
space to complicating narratives of privileged adventuring.
Put another way, the Orvis images reflect a recognition that
environmental awareness is integrally linked to *cultural*
awareness, and to progressive social change.

When I went online it actually took me some sustained
clicking through to get to the page where I could learn more
about the Angling for All pledge. I had to wade past alluring ad
spots calling me, once again, to *plan your fall adventure . . . it's*

*your season for adventure . . . it's time for your fall adventure
. . . gear up for adventure . . .* I felt like I was being trolled by
Orvis as I navigated the website.

Then, I arrived. The informational page leads with this
banner: "Orvis is committed to making fly fishing and the
outdoors more inclusive." Underneath, a bullet-point list of
work underway outlined various initiatives aimed to make
the company "more reflective of American society," including
"increased representation in our online storytelling, social
media, and our catalogs." These are admirable goals, and
the work being done is both practical and intellectual, on
the ground as well as at the organizational level. What
intrigues me about this page is how the motivation comes
from making *fly fishing* more inclusive, but we see how
quickly this is admitted to not be in isolation. It goes hand
in hand with making other realms—from social media to the
vast "outdoors"—just as inclusive. In other words, the real
adventure is not limited to a specific activity (fly-fishing) nor
to a particular special place (a river): it's about social practices
and, well, the *world* writ large. This is a major philosophical
as well as cultural project.

In Giorgio Agamben's pithy study the *Adventure*, he writes
at one point: "We then understand why the event is also always
an event of language and why the adventure is inseparable from
the speech that tells it." Agamben is scouring far older archives
to root out the "original meaning of the term" adventure, and
how it always fuses action and narrative. But we need only
look at these contemporary evocations of adventure to realize
that the event and the telling are inseparable now, as well; and,
in the case of Orvis, adventurers are responsible for a certain
kind of telling: raising awareness of diversity and inequality,
and effecting social change.

So these would seem to be the ends of adventure: not private
trips or achievements in isolation, but working collectively
toward a better, more socially just world, and narrating the
benchmarks of this journey along the way. If adventure is
historically a matter of contingency and risk, the wager here

is definitively social and cultural as much as personal and natural.

These catalog ads are for consumer products, first and foremost. It's easy to dismiss them as merely the icing on the cake of advanced capitalism. But they also beckon outward, to realms that can't be bought and to activities that resist commodification. Even to social justice projects that promise to remake the world, *even* as such a remaking might well upend the very economic structures that are, for now, supporting the systems in place.

As disposable as these catalogs are intended to be, and as deferential as they are to voracious consumer capitalism, they are also enmeshed in fantasies of this far-out *adventure*. And as we have seen, whenever adventure is claimed to be just over the horizon, or accessible only once certain products are procured, in fact there are adventures awaiting before all that. The real adventure, absent in some Orvis pages but overt on others, is to confront and deal with systemic social injustices.

Let's leave the mountains and rivers and head back to the airport, back to Ross Gay and his *Book of Delights*. A relevant entry is called "Tomato on Board":

> What you don't know until you carry a tomato seedling through the airport and onto a plane, is that carrying a tomato seedling through the airport and onto a plane will make people smile at you almost like you're carrying a baby. A quiet baby. I did not know this until today, carrying my little tomato, about three or four inches high in its four-inch plastic starter pot, which my friend Michael gave to me, smirking about how I was going to get it home. Something about this, at first, felt naughty—not comparing a tomato to a baby, but carrying the tomato onto the plane—and so I slid the thing into my bag while going through security, which made them pull the bag for inspection. When the security guy saw it was a tomato he smiled and said, "I don't know how to check that. Have a good day." But I quickly realized that one of its stems (which I almost wrote as "arms") was

broken from the jostling, and it only had four of them, so I decided I better just carry it out in the open. And the shower of love began . . .

Before boarding the final leg of my flight, one of the workers said, "Nice tomato," which I don't think was a come on. And the flight attendant asked about the tomato at least five times, not an exaggeration, every time calling it "my tomato,"—Where's my tomato? How's my tomato? You didn't lose my tomato, did you? She even directed me to an open seat in the exit row—Why don't you guys go sit there and stretch out? I gathered my things and set the lil guy in the window seat so he could look out. When I got my water I poured some into the lil guy's soil. When we got bumpy I put my hand on the lil guy's container, careful not to snap another arm off. And when we landed, and the pilot put the brakes on hard, my arm reflexively went across the seat, holding the lil guy in place, the way my dad's arm would when he had to brake hard in that car without seatbelts to speak of, in one of my very favorite gestures in the encyclopedia of human gestures.

Ross Gay's adventure takes place during an utterly mundane yet magical commercial flight. It is an adventure of cross-species care and attunement to the social. Centered as this story is around a small tomato plant, it also suggests a baseline of environmental awareness: the seedling is carried on board in order to be planted and cared for, later. The adventure is at the airport and up in the air, but also waiting to happen in a ground to come, upon landing. It's also in the narration, the telling of this story which invites us along. It all makes that clichéd slogan *the journey is the destination* very real.

The essayettes that comprise *The Book of Delights* are full of passion and attention to detail—a "joy explosion" as one endorsement on the back cover puts it. But Gay's brief jaunts are also alert to systems and structures, including very much those that involve racism and power dynamics. Even in the relatively upbeat "Tomato on Board," there are still the ambient threats of being profiled at the airport security checkpoint (Gay feels "naughty"), the risk of a plane crashing (the exit row, turbulence), and so on. In other words, these are not just "feel good" compositions, nor are they simply daily gratitudes; sometimes what starts off as a delight turns into a work of mourning, or a wakeup call to how we treat one another (not to mention the planet itself). *The Book of Delights* is a road map for adventures in ordinary contemporary supercharged times.

What do we want from environmental awareness? I've been ranging over some scenes from adventure products, commercial air travel, and contemporary literature to get at this question. If our answer involves making the world better, caring more for the world—then we may have to admit that the "environment" per se shatters like a mirror, or rather, it twists like a Mobius strip back toward us, back onto our *built* world.

In Bruno Latour's book *After Lockdown*, a follow-up to his brilliant pre-pandemic treatise *Down to Earth*, he writes: "We are confined to [Earth] but it's not a prison, it's just that we're *rolled up* in it. Freeing ourselves doesn't mean getting out of it. It means exploring its implications, folds, overlaps, entanglements" (125). In Ross Gay's delights I see this sort of exploration at work, and I see it especially in "Tomato on Board," which both pivots from a commercial flight with all its human self-importance to radically decenter the adventure-premise of air travel. This kind of environmental awareness is about coexisting and casual communications, about listening and responding and remembering, all while bringing a *plant* somewhere else to nurture it, so it will grow. Gay gets positively lost in this air travel experience, and it becomes a different kind of adventure—one that bespeaks a social-ecological ethic.

The ends, or *purpose*, of adventure now should be to work toward a more just society, on a planet that miraculously sustains us. This means not abandoning Earth—sorry, Elon Musk—but recommitting to it in new ways: changing our practices, slowing down, and, in the words of Donna Haraway, "staying with the trouble." If the goal of environmental awareness has been to learn about and better mesh with something like sustainability or resilience—always understood in a dynamic context, with wiggle room for adaptation and change—our adventures must reflect this in new ways, given contemporary extremes in both economic disparities and climate events. And yet counterintuitively, the intensification of circumstances does not call for Big Tech fixes or far-out Futurism.

The adventure, again, is right in front of us—if we dare to look closely and commit to it. This is a familiar yet fresh form of environmental awareness, grounded in the patterns we have made as a species, and open to active revision. If environmental awareness means increasing our care for the planet, then we should be ready to admit that the social is very much part of the planet—indeed, the social makes our planet accessible and legible, as such. So environmental awareness and social justice end up going hand in hand. And when we travel, we may risk getting lost in an airport again—and attending to the limits therein. We might take this planet more seriously, and playfully, as a worthwhile place for our adventures to start, and end.

Conclusion

Some Limits

So what are the limits I've been circuitously arguing for over the course of this book? I'm not entirely sure yet, but some are sliding into focus. Mortality, for one. The limit of a lifetime on Earth. Also, the constraints of time within that duration: hours, days, years. Embracing and working within these periods rather than seeking to elongate or transcend them. But also letting them pass—not trying to "save" time. Adventure is a matter of spending time well. Then seasons, and the cycles that come with them. These are limited phases, and better for the adventures that can take place within. Local and regional boundaries—constructed, flimsy, porous. The backyard, the stream or bog nearby. The nearby is almost always better than any projected beyond. Geographic borders are imaginary or at least fluid, and they tend to go awry when built up, policed, or hypostatized. However, the nearby and an acknowledgment of the possibilities surrounding can reanimate the close-to-home and put a damper on excessive needs for far-flung adventures. Stay close to where you are, more often: pay closer attention to things close by, instead of assuming that textures and details will pop into significance or sublimity once you arrive at a faraway destination. As I'm finishing this book, I receive yet another mailer from Subaru: *Continue your adventure with these tire savings!* But what if the adventure should be continued with fewer car tires involved? We need to accept the limits of automobility: I advocate not so much driving but instead more walking, bicycling, ambling, and other modes of moving slowly across the Earth—if to run into limits and respect them as such. Less travel, then—if only to make infrequent trips more meaningful. And yes: Stay on planet. Put the phone away, especially when walking. Embrace the limits of representation: our stories are always partial and made of flawed material, but this only makes narrative and imagery more interesting and worth treating with care. Consider carefully whether an adventure has succeeded (even modestly) or turned into something else: a mere shopping trip, a mad dash into needless risk, a haughty jaunt. The limits of social life: slower and more sustained conversations, which can lead to environmental awareness and social justice, in tandem. The Möbius strip where environment and culture, humans and nature, are one. (Not a grand Unity, just little ones everywhere.) Limited expressions of adventure might outlive capitalism, and be better for it. The limits of adventure hold the promise of a better planet in the making.

ACKNOWLEDGMENTS

Thank you to Haaris Naqvi for constant support and guidance, once again. Deep gratitude to Alice Marwick for the cover design that made a messy book idea snap into focus for me. Thanks to Rachel Moore, Hali Han, and the rest of the Bloomsbury team—attentive at every turn. Thank you to Anahi Molina for indexing another book! Thank you to Margret Grebowicz and Timothy Morton for reading and believing in an early draft of *Adventure*. Thanks to Ian Bogost, Hillary Eklund, Glen Hannert, KT Thompson, and Mark Yakich, for inspiring and talking through parts of the book. Big thanks to Pardis Mahdavi, Gillian Glaes, Julia Sherman, Ashby Kinch, Chris Dombrowski, Christopher Preston, and the environmental humanities faculty and graduate students at the University of Montana for nuanced and spirited feedback on the final section of the book. Thank you to Nicholas Burtchaell for creating the bibliography and for being a steadfast editorial assistant. Thank you to my editing and publishing students at Loyola in fall 2022—Hannah Bauer, Mae Bennett, Gili Chazoom, Madeline Ditsious, Kenzie Donovan, Chloe Evans, Tiare Perrie, Koee Pipins, Maira Pirzada, Georgia Roberts, Stormy Rogers, Victoria Sosa, Uma Teesdale, and Trinity Wattigney (embedded video!)—for input and critical insights as I finished the book. Finally, overflowing thanks and love to Lara, Julien, Camille, and Vera for being my adventure-mates every single day—here's to many more adventures, hopefully modest and grounded ones, to come.

WORKS CITED

Abbey, Edward. *Desert Solitaire*. Touchstone, 1990.

"Ahead of Tropical Storm Ida, Here's Where to Get Sandbags in the New Orleans Area." *NOLA.com*, August 27, 2021. https://www.nola.com/news/hurricane/article_be61fb7e-d377-11eb-8c43-ff40bfd98344.html.

Allain, Rhett. "Jeff Bezos' Rocket Went to Space—But Not to Orbit: That's Way Harder." *Wired*, 2015. https://www.wired.com/2015/11/getting-into-space-is-much-easier-than-getting-into-orbit/.

Anguiano, Barb. "Blue Origin Space Trip with William Shatner on Board Was a Success." *NPR*, October 14, 2021. https://www.npr.org/2021/10/14/1045904197/blue-origin-space-trip-with-william-shatner-on-board-was-a-success.

Bernstein, Jacob. "Jeff Bezos's Space Style." *The New York Times*, July 21, 2021. https://www.nytimes.com/2021/07/21/style/jeff-bezos-space-image.html.

Blake, William. "Auguries of Innocence." *The Complete Poetry and Prose of William Blake*, ed. David Erdman. University of California Press, 2008.

Bogost, Ian. *Play Anything: The Pleasure of Limits, the Uses of Boredom, and the Secret of Games*. Basic Books, 2016.

"Bonsai Tree 10281." *Lego*, 2022. https://www.lego.com/en-us/product/bonsai-tree-10281.

Bowie, David. "Life on Mars?" *Hunky Dory*, 1973.

Butler, Octavia E. *Dawn*. Grand Central Publishing, 2021.

Butler, Octavia E. *Kindred*. Beacon Press, 2009.

Butler, Octavia E. *Parable of the Sower*. Grand Central Publishing, 2019.

Campanella, Richard. "How Humans Sank New Orleans." *The Atlantic*, 2018. https://www.theatlantic.com/technology/archive/2018/02/how-humans-sank-new-orleans/552323/.

Caplan, Walker. "Octavia Butler Is Now Officially on Mars." *Literary Hub*, March 8, 2021. https://lithub.com/octavia-butler-is -now-officially-on-mars/.

"Captain Kirk: Bezos' Blue Origin to Send William Shatner into Space." *BBC*, October 4, 2021. https://www.bbc.com/news/world -us-canada-58792761.

Chadwick, Douglas. *Four Fifths a Grizzly: A New Perspective on Nature That Just Might Save Us All.* Patagonia, 2021.

"Close-Up of Perseverance Parachute on the Martian Surface." *Jet Propulsion Laboratory*, February 22, 2021. https://www.jpl.nasa .gov/images/pia24336-close-up-of-perseverance-parachute-on-the -martian-surface.

Croft, Hayley. "Hurricane Spaghetti Models." *Cyclocane*, 2021. https://www.cyclocane.com/spaghetti-models/.

Cronon, William. *The Trouble with Wilderness; or, Getting Back to the Wrong Nature.* W.W. Norton & Company, 1995.

Deceptitron. "For Those Who May Be Wondering Where the Original Studio Model of the Refit Enterprise Used in the Films Resides: r/startrek." *Reddit*, August 4, 2016. https://www.reddit .com/r/startrek/comments/4w5zdf/for_those_who_may_be _wondering_where_the_original/.

Dombrowski, Chris. *The River You Touch: Making a Life on Moving Water.* Milkweed, 2022.

Drop Mobility. *Blue Bikes Nola—New Orleans Bike Share*, 2022. https://bluebikesnola.com/.

Eames Office. "Powers of Ten™ (1977)." *YouTube*, Eames Office, August 27, 2010. https://www.youtube.com/watch?v=0fKBhvDjuy0.

Eggers, Dave. *The Every: A Novel.* Knopf Doubleday Publishing Group, 2021.

Eggers, Dave, and Chantal Jahchan. "Opinion | Dave Eggers Created the Google-Amazon Mash-Up of Your Nightmares." *The New York Times*, September 13, 2021. https://www.nytimes.com/2021 /09/13/opinion/sway-kara-swisher-dave-eggers.html.

"Environmental Activism." *Patagonia*, 2021. https://www.patagonia .com/activism/.

Erdrich, Louise. *The Birchbark House.* Hyperion Books for Children, 1999.

"ESA—Mars500: Study Overview." *European Space Agency*. https://www.esa.int/Science_Exploration/Human_and_Robotic _Exploration/Mars500.

Evans, Beau. "46 Tons of Mardi Gras Beads Found in Clogged Catch Basins." *NOLA.com*, January 25, 2018. https://www.nola.com/news/politics/article_37e0ff53-894c-5aed-b4c3-129852582269.html.

Ferociter, Gradatim. "William Shatner and Blue Origin's Audrey Powers to Fly on New Shepard's 18th Mission." *Blue Origin*, 2021. https://www.blueorigin.com/news/shatner-powers-announced-ns18/.

Freeman, James. "Opinion | William Shatner: 'Everybody in the World Needs to Do This.'" *Wall Street Journal*, October 13, 2021. https://www.wsj.com/articles/everybody-in-the-world-needs-to-do-this-11634160156.

Gay, Ross. *The Book of Delights: Essays*. Algonquin Books, 2019.

Glatt, Jana. "Build Your Own Mars Colony." *Laurence King Publishing*, April 20, 2020. https://www.laurenceking.com/products/build-your-own-mars-colony.

Grebowicz, Margret. "Bezos Stole My Space Sex and I Want It Back." *Avidly*, July 20, 2021. https://avidly.lareviewofbooks.org/2021/07/20/bezos-stole-my-space-sex-and-i-want-it-back/.

Greene, Kate. "Living Life at a Distance." *Slate*, 2020. https://slate.com/technology/2020/03/nasa-hi-seas-space-travel-coronavirus-isolation.html.

Herrman, John. "The Meaning of William Shatner's Space Flight with Blue Origin." *The New York Times*, October 13, 2021. https://www.nytimes.com/2021/10/07/style/shatner-bezos-blue-origin.html.

Jarvey, Natalie. "'Star Trek Beyond:' Amazon CEO Jeff Bezos Shares Video in Alien Makeup for His Cameo." *The Hollywood Reporter*, July 20, 2016. https://www.hollywoodreporter.com/movies/movie-news/star-trek-beyond-jeff-bezos-913039/.

Kerouac, Jack. *Big Sur*. Penguin Publishing Group, 1992.

Koren, Marina. "The Cost of William Shatner's 'Most Profound Experience.'" *The Atlantic*, October 13, 2021. https://www.theatlantic.com/science/archive/2021/10/william-shatner-blue-origin/620370/.

Koren, Marina. "Elon Musk Is Maybe, Actually, Strangely Going to Do This Mars Thing." *The Atlantic*, May 6, 2021. https://www.theatlantic.com/science/archive/2021/05/elon-musk-spacex-starship-launch/618781/.

Koren, Marina. "Elon Musk Must Be Pretty Relieved." *The Atlantic*, September 18, 2021. https://www.theatlantic.com

/science/archive/2021/09/spacex-inspiration-4-splashdown
/620128/.

Koren, Marina. "A Historic Docking, 250 Miles Above Earth." *The Atlantic*, May 31, 2020. https://www.theatlantic.com/science /archive/2020/05/historic-journey-international-space-station -spacex-nasa/612427/.

Koren, Marina. "Scientists Really, Really Want a Piece of Mars." *The Atlantic*, February 18, 2021. https://www.theatlantic.com/science/ archive/2021/02/mars-rover-peserverance-rocks-shipping/618039/.

Koren, Marina. "SpaceX's Private Astronauts Are Flying Higher Than the Space Station." *The Atlantic*, September 15, 2021. https://www.theatlantic.com/science/archive/2021/09/spacex -inspiration4-launch/620093/.

Kramer, Andrew E. "Russia to Open New Frontier in Space, Shooting First Full-Length Movie." *The New York Times*, October 15, 2021. https://www.nytimes.com/2021/09/16/world/ europe/russia-movie-space.html.

Latour, Bruno. *After Lockdown: A Metamorphosis*. Translated by Julie Rose, Wiley, 2021.

Lopez, Barry. *Field Notes: The Grace Note of the Canyon Wren*. Knopf Doubleday Publishing Group, 2004.

"MARS-500." *Wikipedia*, 2020. https://en.wikipedia.org/wiki/MARS -500.

"Mars Landing." *Wikipedia*, 2021. https://en.wikipedia.org/wiki/ Mars_landing.

McCloud, Cheryl. "National Hurricane Center's Cone of Uncertainty Explained." *The News-Press*, June 30, 2021. https:// www.news-press.com/story/weather/hurricane/2021/06/30/nhc -cone-uncertainty-concerned-explained-what-is-it-explanations -answers-common-questions/7383995002/.

McCormack, Simon. "Jeff Bezos' Rocket Looks Like a Penis." *HuffPost*, April 30, 2015. https://www.huffpost.com/entry/jeff -bezos-rocket-penis_n_7182914.

McDowell, Jonathan. "Highlights from William Shatner's Blue Origin Rocket Trip to Space." *The New York Times*, October 13, 2021. https://www.nytimes.com/live/2021/10/13/science/blue -origin-william-shatner.

Messeri, Lisa. *Placing Outer Space: An Earthly Ethnography of Other Worlds*. Duke University Press, 2016. https://www .dukeupress.edu/placing-outer-space.

Meyer, Robinson. "The Latest IPCC Report Is a Catastrophe." *The Atlantic*, August 9, 2021. https://www.theatlantic.com/science/archive/2021/08/latest-ipcc-report-catastrophe/619698/.

Meyer, Robinson. "We're Hitting the Limits of Hurricane Preparedness." *The Atlantic*, August 29, 2021. https://www.theatlantic.com/science/archive/2021/08/hurricane-ida-end-of-hurricane-preparedness/619926/.

Migliozzi, Blacki et al. "Map: Where Ida Has Left Louisiana and Mississippi Without Power (Published 2021)." *The New York Times*, August 26, 2021. https://www.nytimes.com/interactive/2021/us/hurricane-ida-tracker.html.

Migliozzi, Blacki, and Hiroko Tabuchi. "Satellite Images Find 'Substantial' Oil Spill in Gulf After Ida (Published 2021)." *The New York Times*, September 4, 2021. https://www.nytimes.com/2021/09/04/climate/oil-spill-hurricane-ida.html.

"Motherhood Is the Greatest Adventure of All: Angelina Jolie." *DNA India*, November 21, 2013. https://www.dnaindia.com/entertainment/report-motherhood-is-the-greatest-adventure-of-all-angelina-jolie-1410986.

Mull, Amanda. "There's a Perfect Number of Days to Work from Home, and It's 2." *The Atlantic*, May 10, 2021. https://www.theatlantic.com/health/archive/2021/05/work-from-home-2-days-a-week/618841/.

Musk, Elon. "Missions: Earth." *SpaceX*, 2020. https://www.spacex.com/human-spaceflight/earth/index.html.

Musk, Elon. "Missions: Mars." *SpaceX*, 2020. https://www.spacex.com/human-spaceflight/mars/.

Musk, Elon. "Starship." *SpaceX*, 2021. https://www.spacex.com/vehicles/starship/.

"NASA Space Shuttle Discovery 10283." *Lego*, 2022. https://www.lego.com/en-us/product/nasa-space-shuttle-discovery-10283.

"NASA's Perseverance Drives on Mars' Terrain for First Time." *Jet Propulsion Laboratory*, March 5, 2021. https://www.jpl.nasa.gov/news/nasas-perseverance-drives-on-mars-terrain-for-first-time.

"Nathan Sawaya | LEGO Sculpture | Art of the Brick." *Avant Gallery*, 2020. https://avantgallery.com/nathan-sawaya/.

National Aeronautics and Space Administration. "NASA Ingenuity Mars Helicopter Prepares for First Flight." March 23, 2021. https://www.nasa.gov/press-release/nasa-ingenuity-mars-helicopter-prepares-for-first-flight.

"NOAA Hurricane Hunters | Office of Marine and Aviation Operations." *NOAA OMAO*, 2022. https://www.omao.noaa.gov/learn/aircraft-operations/about/hurricane-hunters.

O'Hare, Maureen. "Boom Supersonic Aims to Fly 'Anywhere in the World in Four Hours for $100.'" *CNN*, May 18, 2021. http://edition.cnn.com/travel/article/boom-supersonic-four-hours-100-bucks/index.html.

Okwodu, Janelle. "What Does Star Trek Have to Do with Fashion? A Lot, Actually." *Vogue*, July 22, 2016. https://www.vogue.com/article/star-trek-surprising-fashion-influence.

Organic Vegetarian Traditional Refried Beans, Light in Sodium. Amy's Kitchen, 2021. https://www.amys.com/our-foods/organic-vegetarian-traditional-refried-beans-light-in-sodium.

Ortlepp, Anke. *Jim Crow Terminals: The Desegregation of American Airports.* University of Georgia Press, 2017.

"Overview—NASA Mars." *NASA's Mars Exploration Program*, 2022. https://mars.nasa.gov/programmissions/overview/.

Owen, David. "Game of Thrones: How Airlines Woo the One Per Cent." *The New Yorker*, April 14, 2014. https://www.newyorker.com/magazine/2014/04/21/game-of-thrones.

Owens, Jay. "As Above, so Below: A Review of Space Forces: A Critical History of Life in Space by Fred Scharmen." *Ancillary Review of Books*, February 2, 2022. https://ancillaryreviewofbooks.org/2022/02/02/as-above-so-below-a-review-of-space-forces/.

Patchett, Ann. *These Precious Days: Essays.* Harper Collins, 2021.

Robinson, Kim Stanley. *Red Mars.* Random House Worlds, 2021. https://www.penguinrandomhouse.com/books/156201/red-mars-by-kim-stanley-robinson/.

Robinson, Kim Stanley. *The Ministry for the Future.* Hachette/Orbit, 2020.

Russell, Andrew, and Lee Vinsel. "Whitey on Mars: Elon Musk and the Rise of Silicon Valley's Strange Trickle-Down Science." *Aeon*, February 1, 2017. https://aeon.co/essays/is-a-mission-to-mars-morally-defensible-given-todays-real-needs.

Schaberg, Christopher. "How Much Has Environmental Awareness Expanded over the Past Decade?" *Terrain*, August 2, 2021. https://www.terrain.org/2021/reviews-reads/ecological-thought/.

Scharmen, Fred. *Space Settlements.* Columbia Books on Architecture and the City, 2019.

Schleifstein, Mark. "Hurricane Ida to be Catastrophic Category
    4 Storm Blasting Most of Louisiana Coast." *NOLA.com* [New
    Orleans], August 27, 2021. https://www.nola.com/news/hurricane
    /article_e58cb122-0756-11ec-9d61-d3e4491f7455.html.
Scott-Heron, Gil. "Whitey on the Moon." *Small Talk at 125th and
    Lenox*, 1970.
Shelley, Percy Bysshe. "Ozymandias." *Shelley's Poetry and Prose*,
    1977.
Skibba, Ramin. "How to Optimise Your Headspace on a Mission to
    Mars." *Aeon*, 2020. https://aeon.co/ideas/how-to-optimise-your
    -headspace-on-a-mission-to-mars.
Solon, Olivia. "Elon Musk: We Must Colonise Mars to Preserve Our
    Species in a Third World War." *The Guardian*, March 12, 2018.
    https://www.theguardian.com/technology/2018/mar/11/elon
    -musk-colonise-mars-third-world-war.
"Space Shuttle Adventure 31117." *Lego*, 2021. https://www.lego
    .com/en-us/product/space-shuttle-adventure-31117.
SpaceX. "Starship Users Guide." *SpaceX*, March 2020. https://www
    .spacex.com/media/starship_users_guide_v1.pdf.
Steere, Tania. "Virgin Galactic Announces First Fully Crewed
    Spaceflight." *Virgin*, 2021. https://www.virgin.com/about-virgin/
    latest/virgin-galactic-announces-first-fully-crewed-spaceflight.
Stirone, Shannon. "Mars Is a Hellhole." *The Atlantic*, 2021. https://
    www.theatlantic.com/ideas/archive/2021/02/mars-is-no-earth
    /618133/.
Tayeb, Zahra. "NASA Is Paying People to Live in 3D-Printed
    Martian Habitat for a Year." *Business Insider*, August 8, 2021.
    https://www.businessinsider.com/nasa-mars-3d-printed-martian
    -habitat-paid-volunteers-space-2021-8.
Tolle, Madeline. "Documenting Los Angeles's Unlikely Urban
    Fishermen." *The New York Times*, March 15, 2022. https://www
    .nytimes.com/2022/01/31/travel/urban-fishing-los-angeles.html.
Tumin, Remy. "Riders Catch a Little Too Much Air on a Detroit
    Slide." *The New York Times*, August 26, 2022. https://www
    .nytimes.com/2022/08/26/us/belle-isle-giant-slide-detroit.html.
Wordsworth, William. "I Wandered Lonely as a Cloud." 1807.
Zimmer, Carl. "The Lost History of One of the World's Strangest
    Science Experiments (Published 2019)." *The New York Times*,
    March 29, 2019. https://www.nytimes.com/2019/03/29/sunday
    -review/biosphere-2-climate-change.html.

Social Media

Cantrell, LaToya (@mayorcantrell). "Message from @
Swbneworleans: We Are Responding to Diesel Spillage in the
Lafitte Canal from Powering Generators & Are in the Process of
Isolating the Oil. To Protect Our Environment & Water Systems,
Please Do Not Pour Oil, Diesel or Any Cleaning Materials down
the Storm Drains." *Twitter*, October 29, 2020. https://twitter.com
/mayorcantrell/status/1321870520342765569?s=20.

Eon (@EthanHeyns). "Yo Mark Watney's Still There! At Least He'll
Be Able to Fly Around Ingenuity." *Twitter*, February 18, 2021.
https://twitter.com/EthanHeyns/status/1362517533752889344?s
=20.

Everyday Astronaut (@Erdayastronaut). "Here's a Scale Comparison
I Never Really Saw Coming!!! Makes You Realize JUST
HOW BIG Starship Will Be! Pictured is the Falcon 9 w/Crew
Dragon, Atlas V w/Starliner, Soyuz, Starship, a Boeing 747-8F
and a Boeing 737-800. YES, These Are to Scale!!!" *Twitter*,
March 16, 2020. https://twitter.com/Erdayastronaut/status
/1239595527114838018?s=20.

Groff, David (@_davidgroff). *Instagram*, February 18, 2021. https://
www.instagram.com/p/CLdBYGtBvt6/?igshid=nfpw9ovue8gf.

McBride, Matt (@Matthew67052126). "The @uscg National
Response Center Includes a Report Filed Just after Midnight
10/29/20 of a Diesel Tank Overflowing into Storm Drains at
3000 Perdido St Due to Hurricane #Zeta. That Address Is
Orleans Parish Prison. The Storm Drains from There Lead to
DPS 2 and the Lafitte Canal." *Twitter*, November 6, 2020. https://
twitter.com/Matthew67052126/status/1324747035841568771?s
=20.

NASA's Perseverance Mars Rover (@NASAPersevere). *Twitter*.
https://twitter.com/NASAPersevere.

Nye, Bill (@BillNye). "It's Out of This World!" *Twitter*, February 22,
2021. https://twitter.com/BillNye/status/1363995014217355267
?s=20.

SpaceX (@SpaceX). "The 737-Sized First Stage Propellant Tank for
a Future Falcon 9 Nears Completion at Our Hawthorne, CA
Headquarters." *Twitter*, January 19, 2012. https://twitter.com/
SpaceX/status/160114519887200257?s=20.

Wolfram (@WolframResearch). "@NASA Recently Announced
     That the Parachute of Its Perseverance Mars Rover Contained
     a Hidden Message. Ahmed Elbanna Shares How to Recreate
     and Decode the Binary Message, and Explains How One Can
     Create Their Own Encoded Message: https://wolfr.am/TR1IP8ob
     #daremightythings." *Twitter*, March 8, 2021. https://twitter.com/
     WolframResearch/status/1368987302601621506?s=20.

INDEX

Select Praise for Christopher Schaberg's Previous Books with Bloomsbury

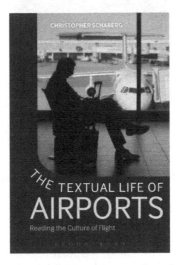

The Textual Life of Airports: Reading the Culture of Flight (2012)

"Wonderful."
—Peter Adey, author of *Aerial Life: Spaces, Mobilities, Affects*

"The Pulitzer Prize-winning journalist and former Masterpiece Theatre host Russell Wayne Baker once lamented that the public imagines reading poetry to be worse than carrying heavy luggage through Chicago's O'Hare airport. In *The Textual Life of Airports*, Schaberg offers a shrewd response: the airport is the poetry."
—Ian Bogost, Professor of Media Studies at Washington University in St. Louis, and author of *Play Anything*

The End of Airports (2015)

". . .[a] well-fuelled study of air travel's fading profile
in our digitally transported age."
—Nathan Heller, *The New Yorker*

"Tracing speculative paths around and through airports and
commercial flight, *The End of Airports* finds new ways to think
about, among other things, drones, airport/aircraft seating,
weather, jet bridges, viral stories about flight, tensions with new
media expectations and technologies, and seatback pockets.
A fascinating read for anyone interested in airports and
airplanes, but also for readers of cultural studies, media studies,
and creative nonfiction."
—Kathleen C. Stewart, Professor of Anthropology,
The University of Texas at Austin, USA, and author of
Ordinary Affects

Airportness: The Nature of Flight (2017)

"Slim and elegant . . . Schaberg has an intuitive way for us to cruise over this landscape of theoretical hills and valleys. He uses the first-person voice to recreate an average journey made by air."
—Times Literary Supplement

"*Airportness* is an insightful, witty guide to the ecologies of Earth's strange new habitat. A Thoreau not of Concord, but of the concourse, Schaberg writes with boundless curiosity for the many layers of meaning and contradiction within the physical and mental space of airports."
—David George Haskell, Professor of Biology, University of the South, USA, and author of *The Songs of Trees* and Pulitzer finalist *The Forest Unseen*

"With deep insight and a singular brilliance, Christopher Schaberg takes the reader on a journey from curb to curb, chastising us for our indifference to cloudscapes, rekindling our wonder for liftoff, asking us to reckon with airport as metaphor for late-stage capitalism, for American identity, for the last vestiges of faith, even, ironically, for what we call home. Part razor-sharp critique, part advanced elegy for a doomed mode of transportation, *Airportness* is finally a declaration of love for a threatened land(sky)scape, an imperative to remain awake and alive."
—Pam Houston, Professor of English, UC Davis, USA, and author of *Deep Creek: Finding Hope in the High Country*

The Work of Literature in an Age of Post-Truth (2018)

"*The Work of Literature in an Age of Post-Truth* captures the essence of what it is like to experience the wildness of the 21st century as an observant, thinking human. The banalities of everyday life mix here with the political urgencies and mediatic confusion of our age. Schaberg has sketched a convincing portrait of this unsettling moment."
—Christy Wampole, Professor of French, Princeton University, USA, and author of *Rootedness: The Ramifications of a Metaphor*

"Schaberg takes readers to various locations, allowing them to eavesdrop on his thoughts . . . Schaberg soars when talking about language."
—Publishers Weekly

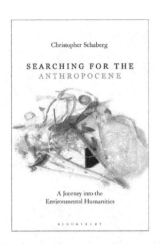

Searching for the Anthropocene: A Journey into the Environmental Humanities (2019)

"[Schaberg] makes sharp observations on the Anthropocene's reflection across the span of human projects, from the most insignificant to the most magnificent. Schaberg divides the book into two parts: 'Home Sick' and 'Jet Lag.' . . . Each part comprises multiple short pieces that speak to large ecological themes. Each piece is a treat of ecological wisdom, self-reflection, critical imagination, and elegant writing. *Searching for the Anthropocene* carries the ecocritical lessons beyond Michigan and midwestern America to the continental US and beyond, demonstrating how the human ecological footprint has grown into the Anthropocene. An invaluable resource for students and scholars of ecocriticism, critical theory, and environmental studies. Summing Up: Highly recommended. All readers."
—Choice

"Christopher Schaberg wanders Michigan's north woods and far flung airfields to lyrically ferret out the absurdity of the 'Anthropocene.' Schaberg shows how Homo sapiens are no longer in charge of anything, despite our terrifying and irreversible wounding of a planet reeling from climate change. It's a coin-toss whether there will be anything around at the end of the next decade capable of reading this fine book."
—Doug Peacock, author of *Grizzly Years* and *Was it Worth It? A Wilderness Warrior's Long Trail Home*

Pedagogy of the Depressed (2022)

"How do you teach through trauma? All college instructors have found themselves facing this question in recent days, but few with the insight and poignancy of Christopher Schaberg. *Pedagogy of the Depressed* provides both diagnosis and balm for those anxious about the possibilities for higher education in the midst of climate change and active shooter events and pandemic response and budgetary collapse, a profound reckoning with the conditions of learning today."
—Kathleen Fitzpatrick, Director of Digital Humanities and Professor of English, Michigan State University, USA, and author of *Generous Thinking: A Radical Approach to Saving the University*